Classical Guitar Tunes

BEAUTIFUL AMERICAN AIRS AND BALLADS

by Tanja Mirić

The Corona model Western Red Cedar Mountain guitar image on the cover is courtesy of Prenkert Guitars.

I0808774

WWW.MELBAY.COM

Preface

Thank you for your interest in *Beautiful American Airs and Ballads.*

When company president and editor-in-chief William Bay suggested I arrange these pieces, I must confess I had little familiarity with 19th century American songs. Upon further research, I discovered a treasure trove of beautiful melodies well suited to the guitar.

My goal was to make these arrangements accessible to intermediate guitarists. The pieces use a variety of guitar-friendly keys, open strings, common arpeggio patterns, familiar harmonic progressions and in some instances— key changes. Possibly, they may provide inspiration and a model for guitarists to create their own arrangements.

Selecting perhaps three pieces as a set, these arrangements are suitable for recitals as well as encores. In my own concerts, I have performed a selection of them and received very favorable audience feedback.

Acknowledgements

I would be remiss if I did not express my gratitude to Dr. John Ingwerson, my wonderful guitar teacher and retired professor, for his proofreading and insightful fingering concepts.

Contents

Jeanie with the Light Brown Hair

Stephen Foster
(1826-1864)
arr. Tanja Mirić

Andante ♩ = 90

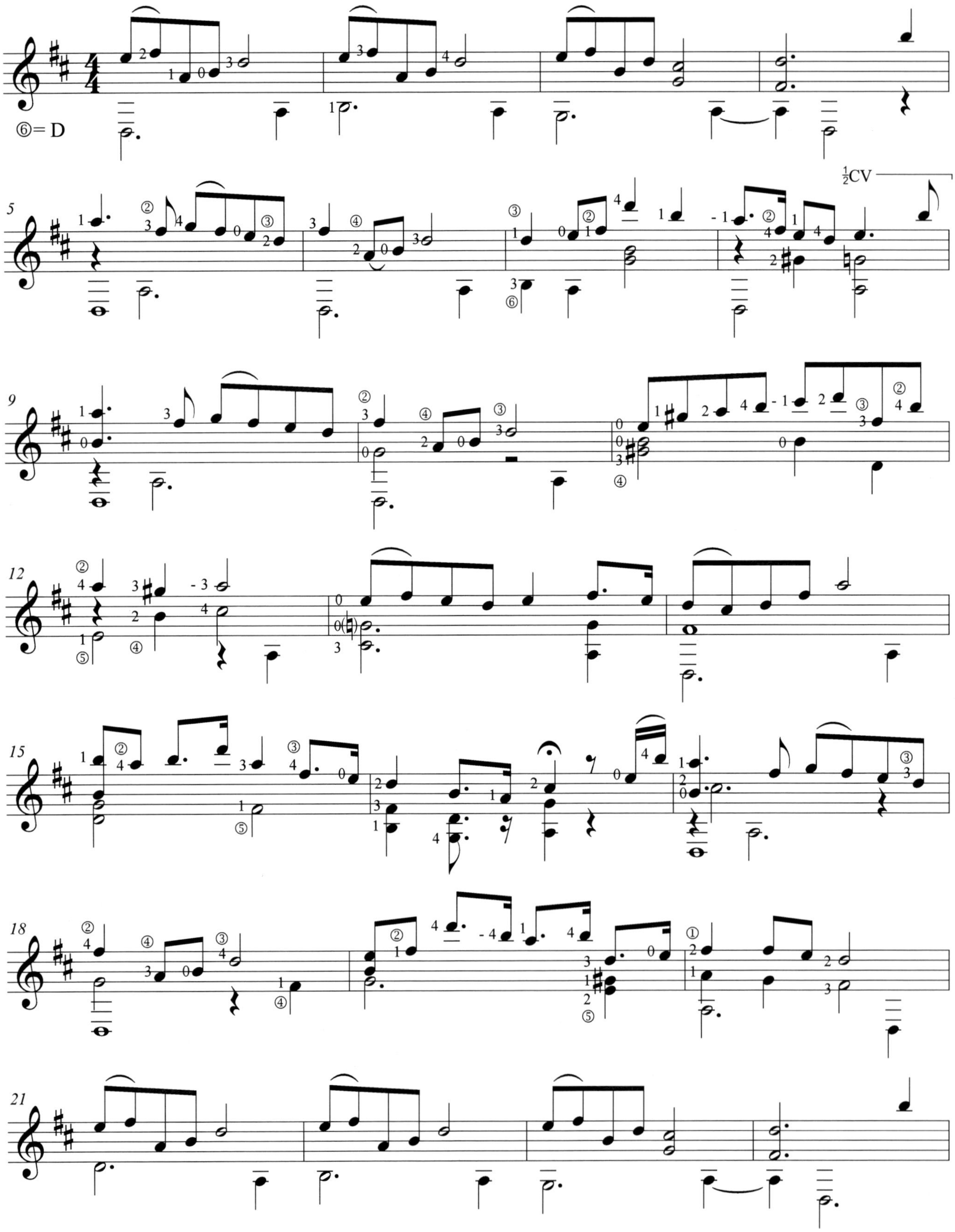

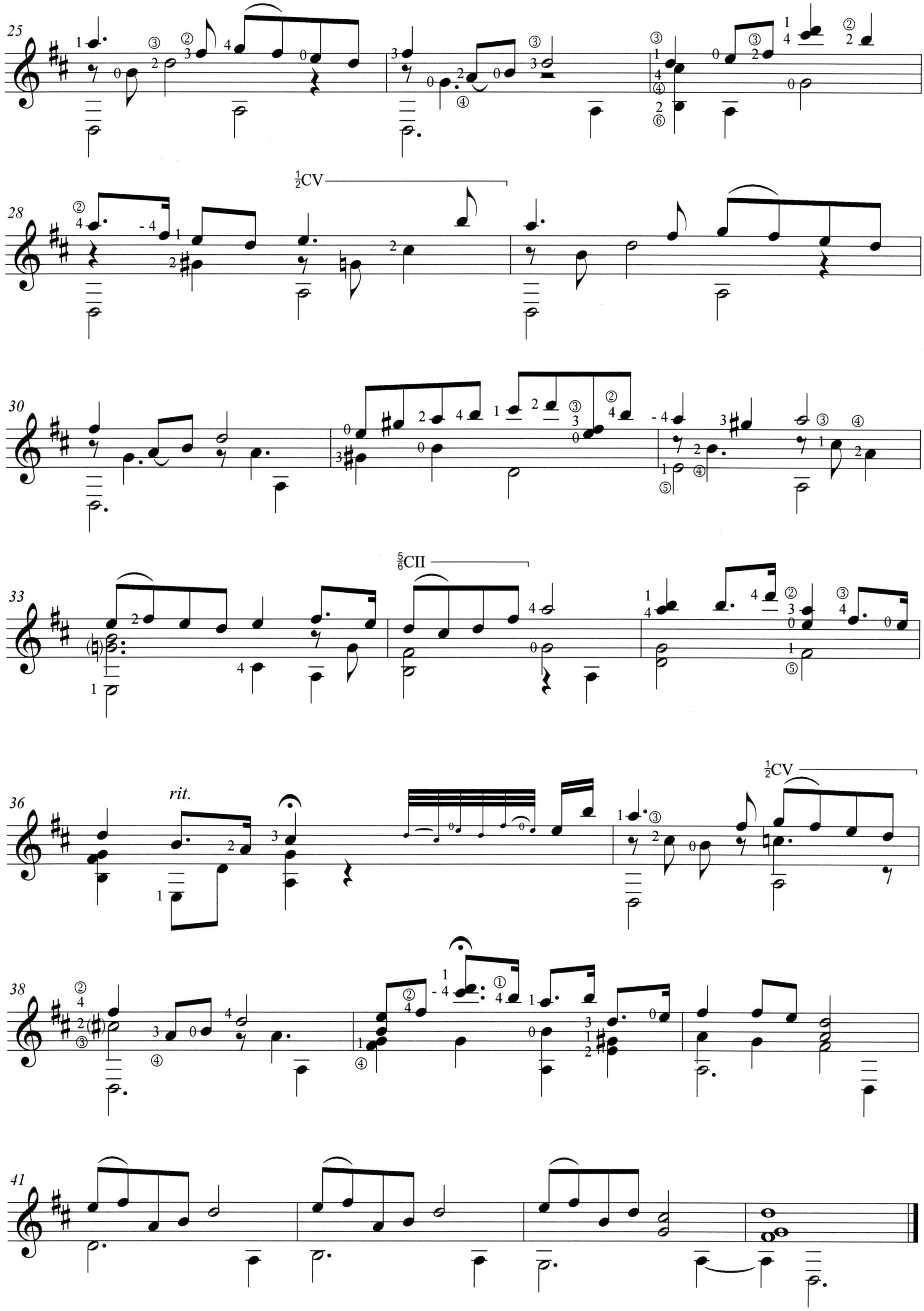
25
28
½CV
30
33
5/6CII
36
rit.
½CV
38
41

Just Before the Battle, Mother

Civil War Song
George F. Root (1820-1895)
arr. Tanja Mirić

Tenderly ♩ = 85

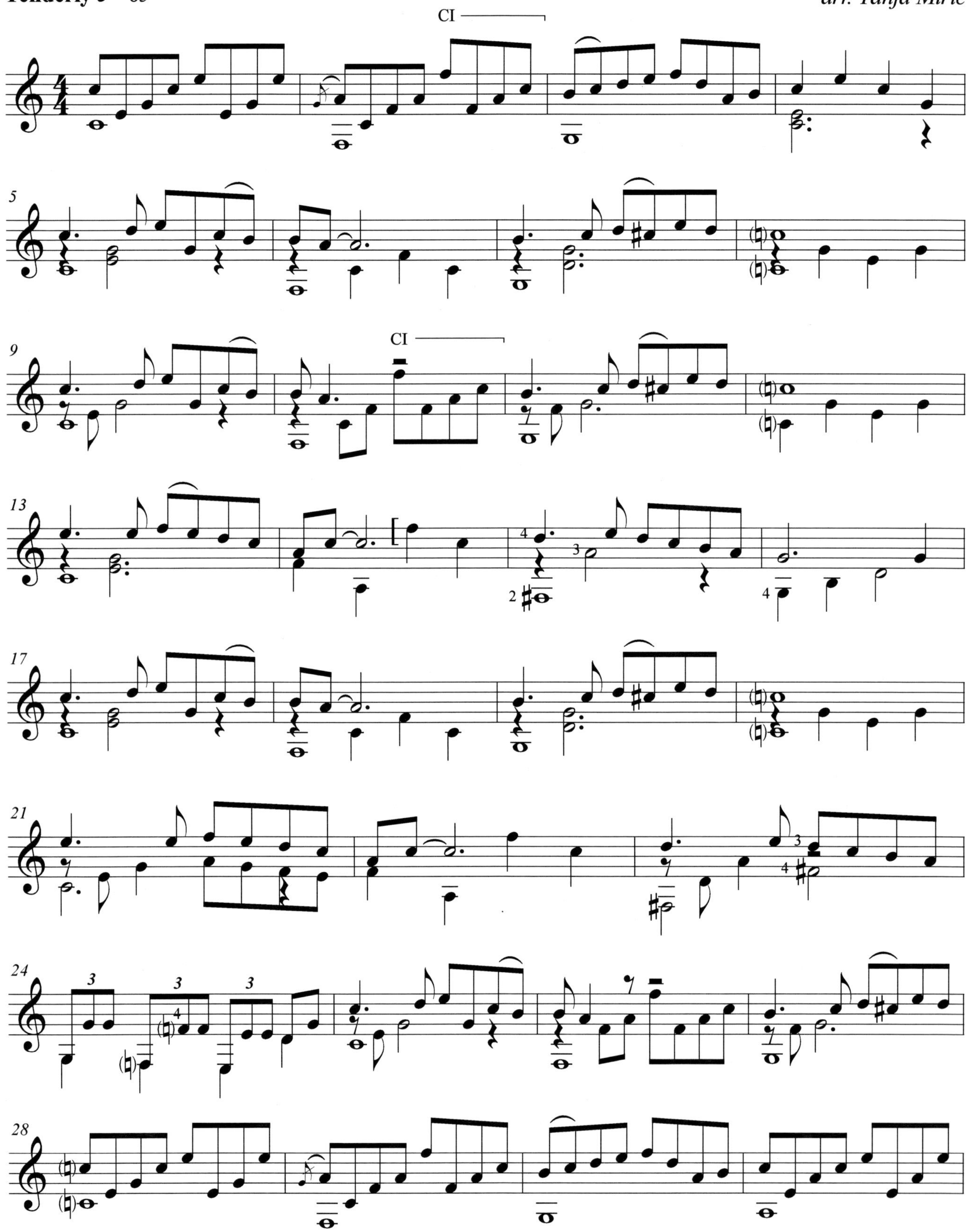

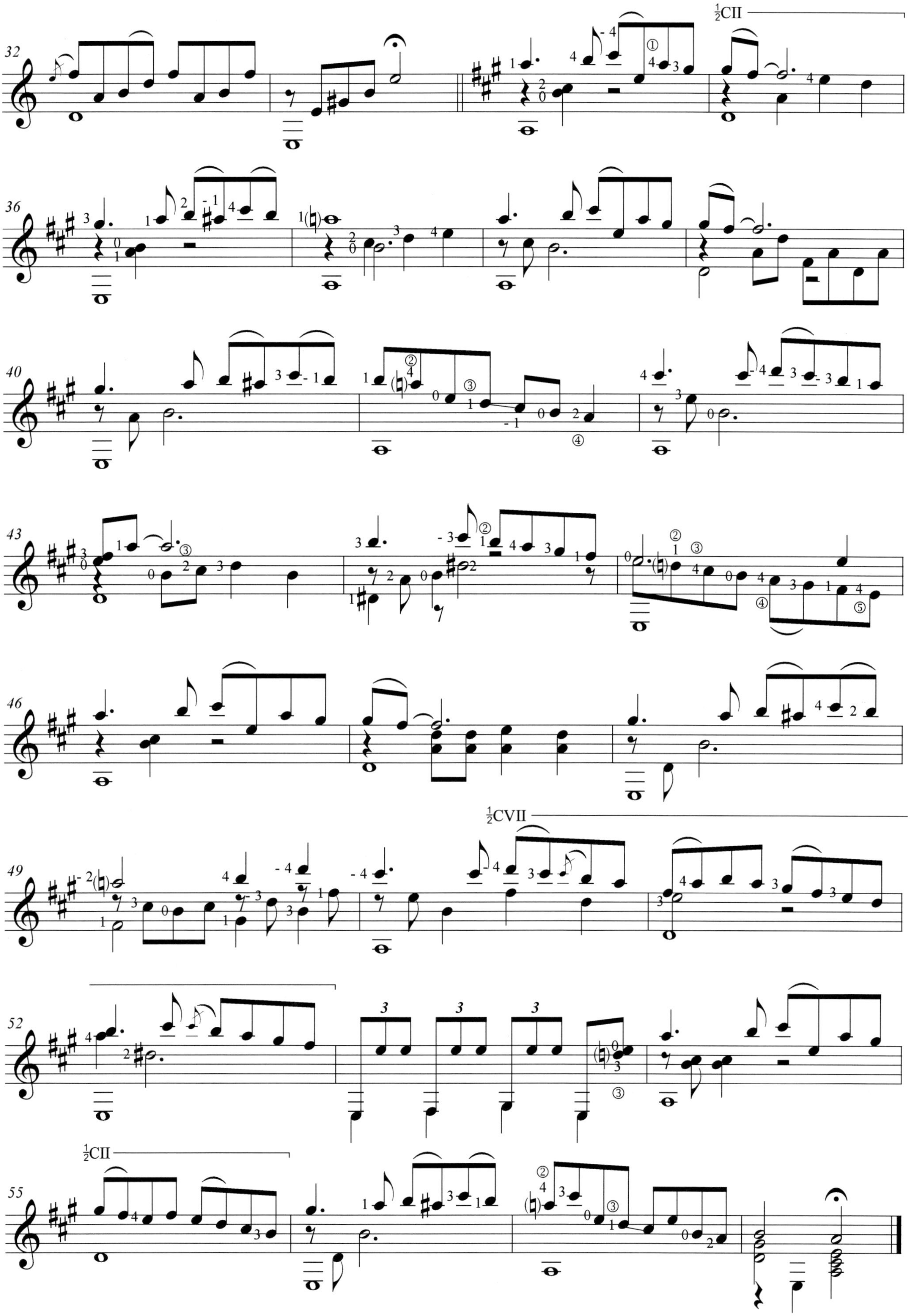
½CII
½CVII
½CII

Darling Nelly Gray

B. R. Hanby
(1833-1867)
arr. Tanja Mirić

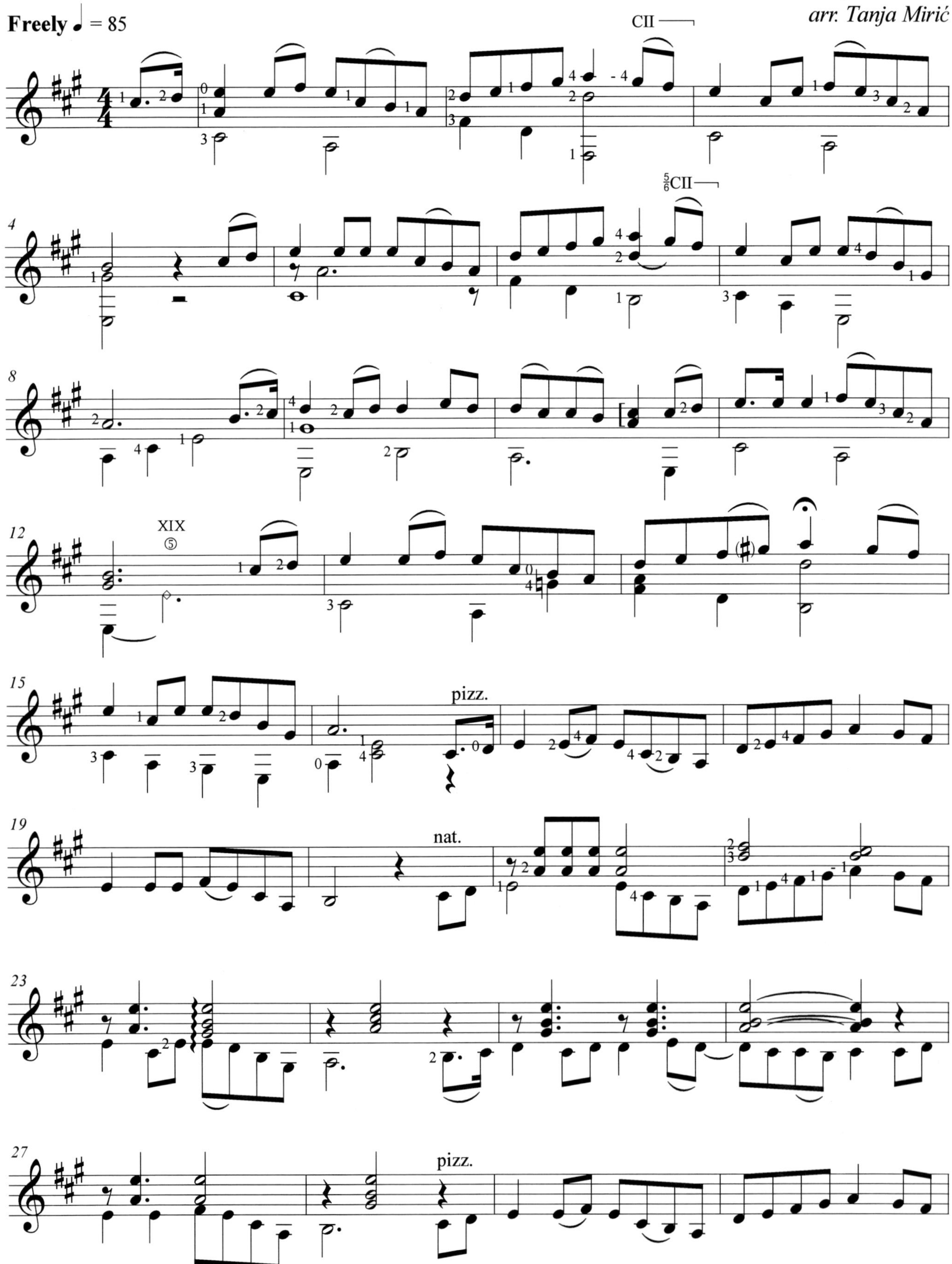

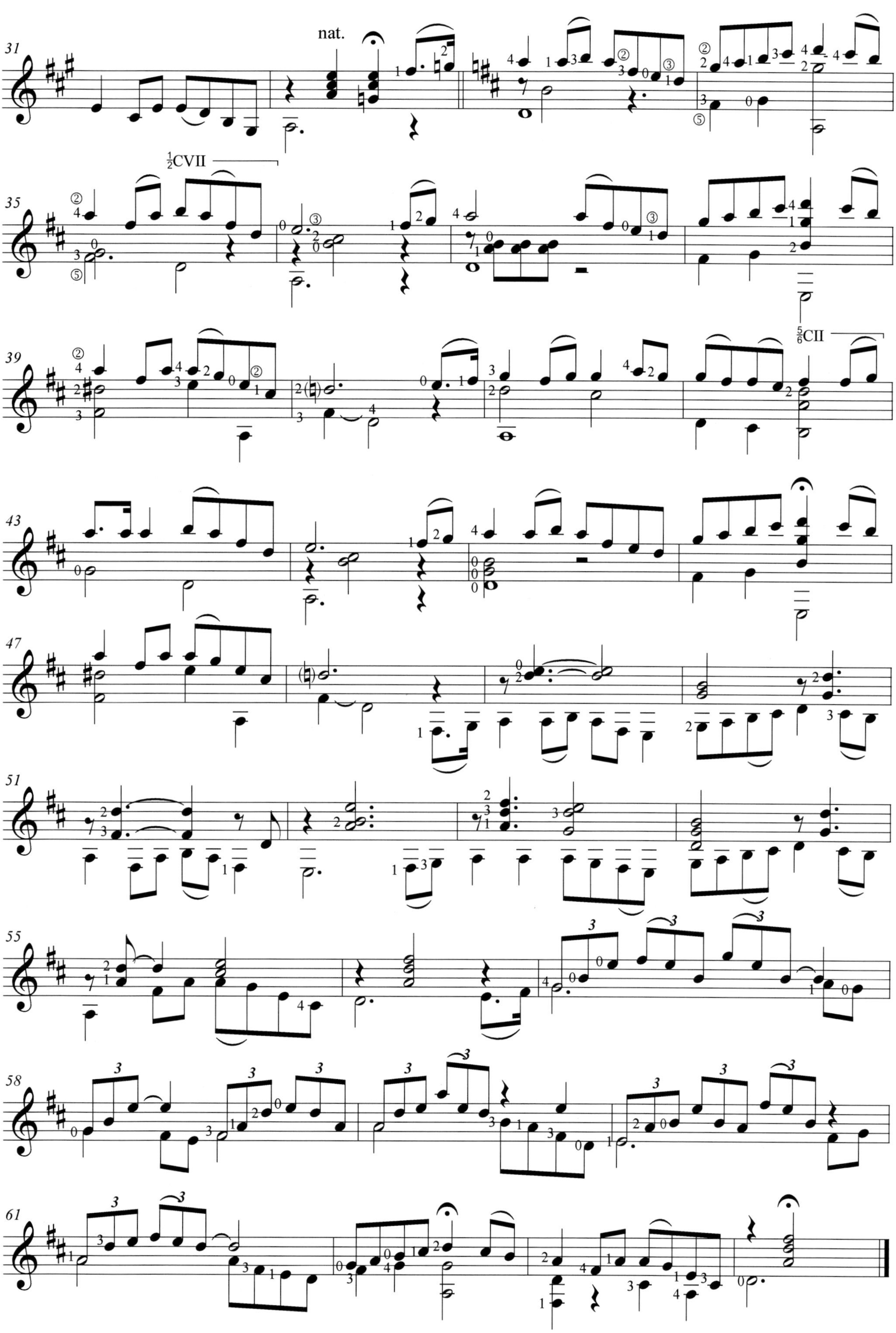
nat.
½CVII
5/6CII

Hard Times Come Again No More

Stephen Foster
(1826-1864)
arr. Tanja Mirić

Freely ♩ = 74

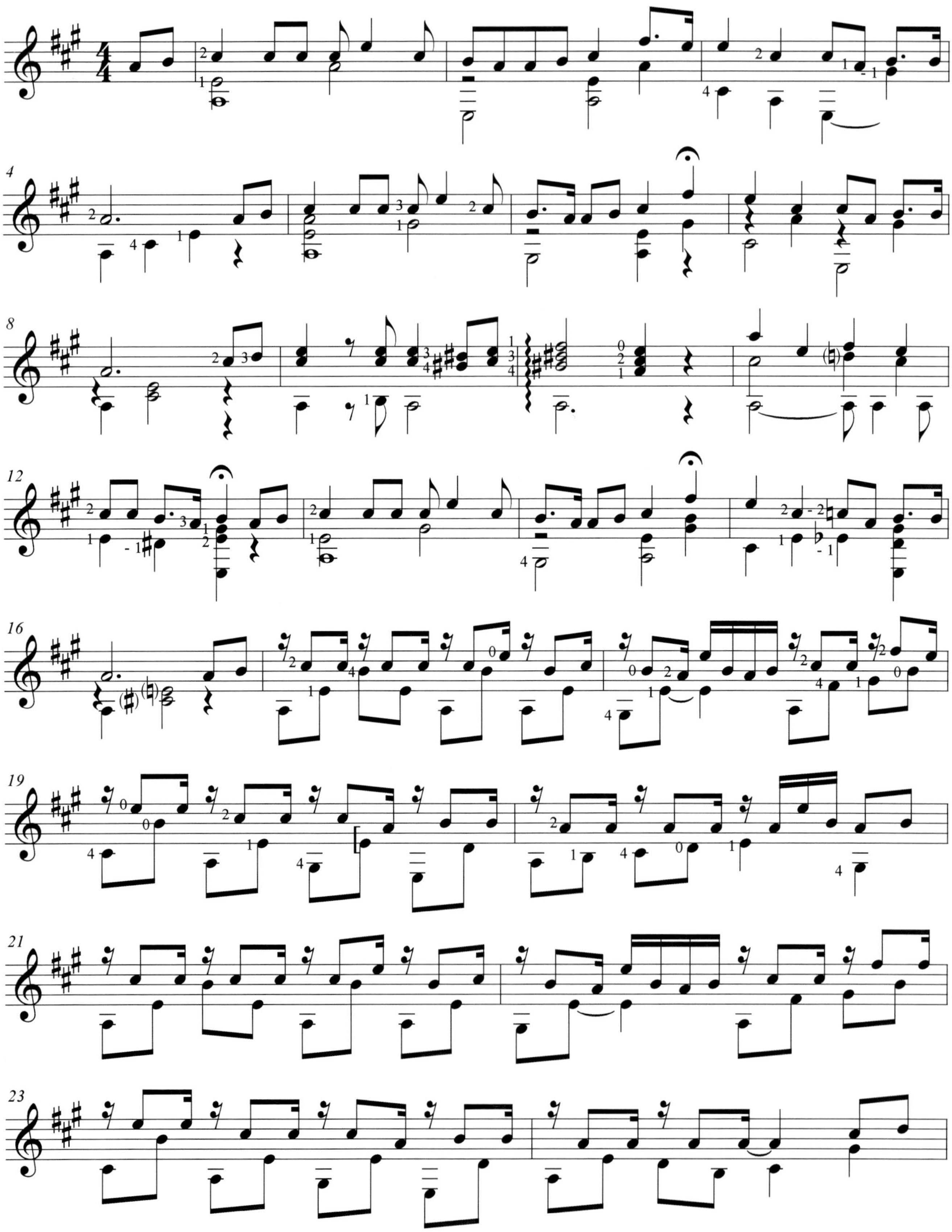

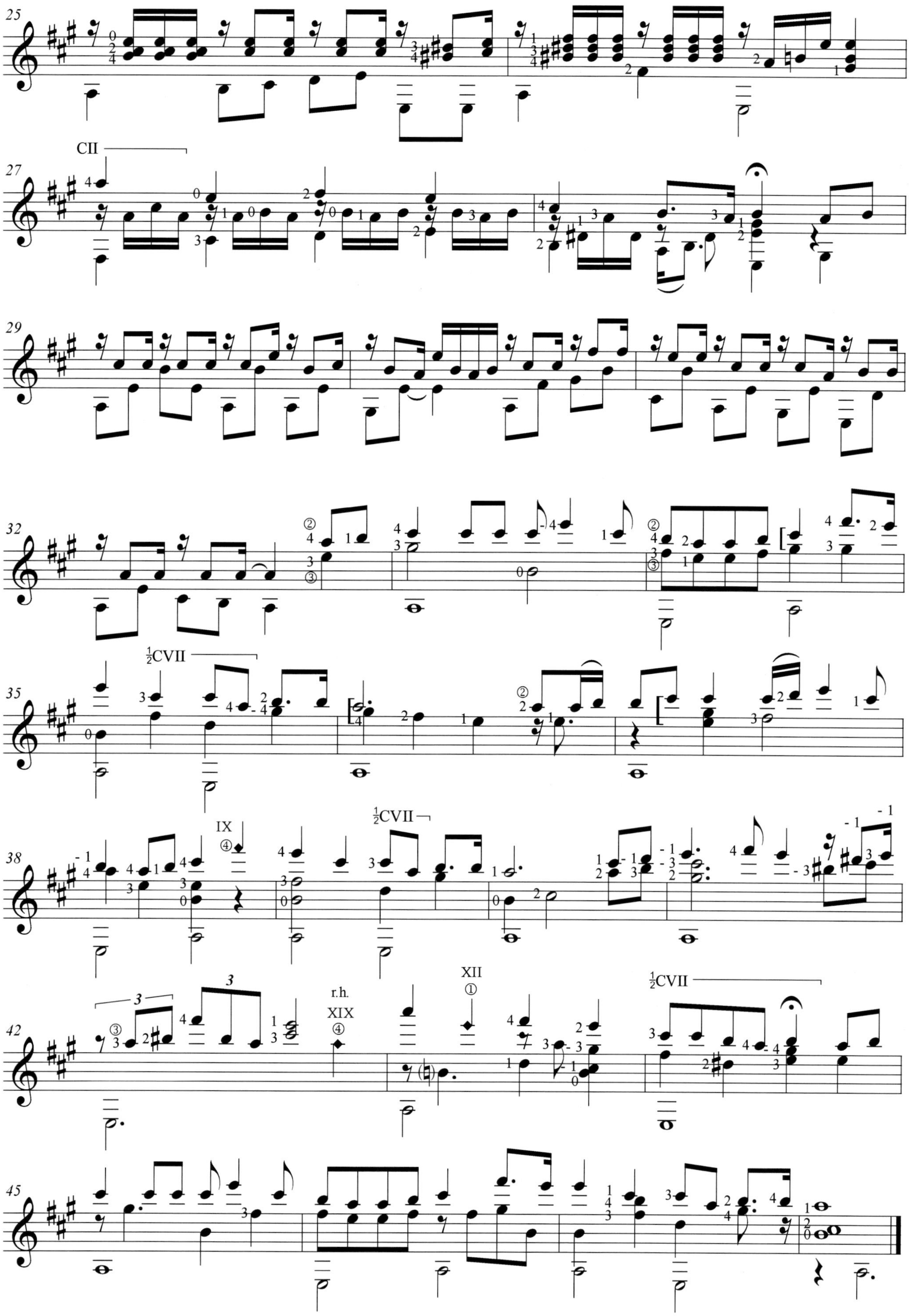
25
27
CII
29
32
35
½CVII
38
IX
½CVII
42
r.h.
XIX
XII
½CVII
45

Beautiful Dreamer

Stephen C. Foster
(1826-1864)
arr. Tanja Mirić

Moderato ♩. = 60

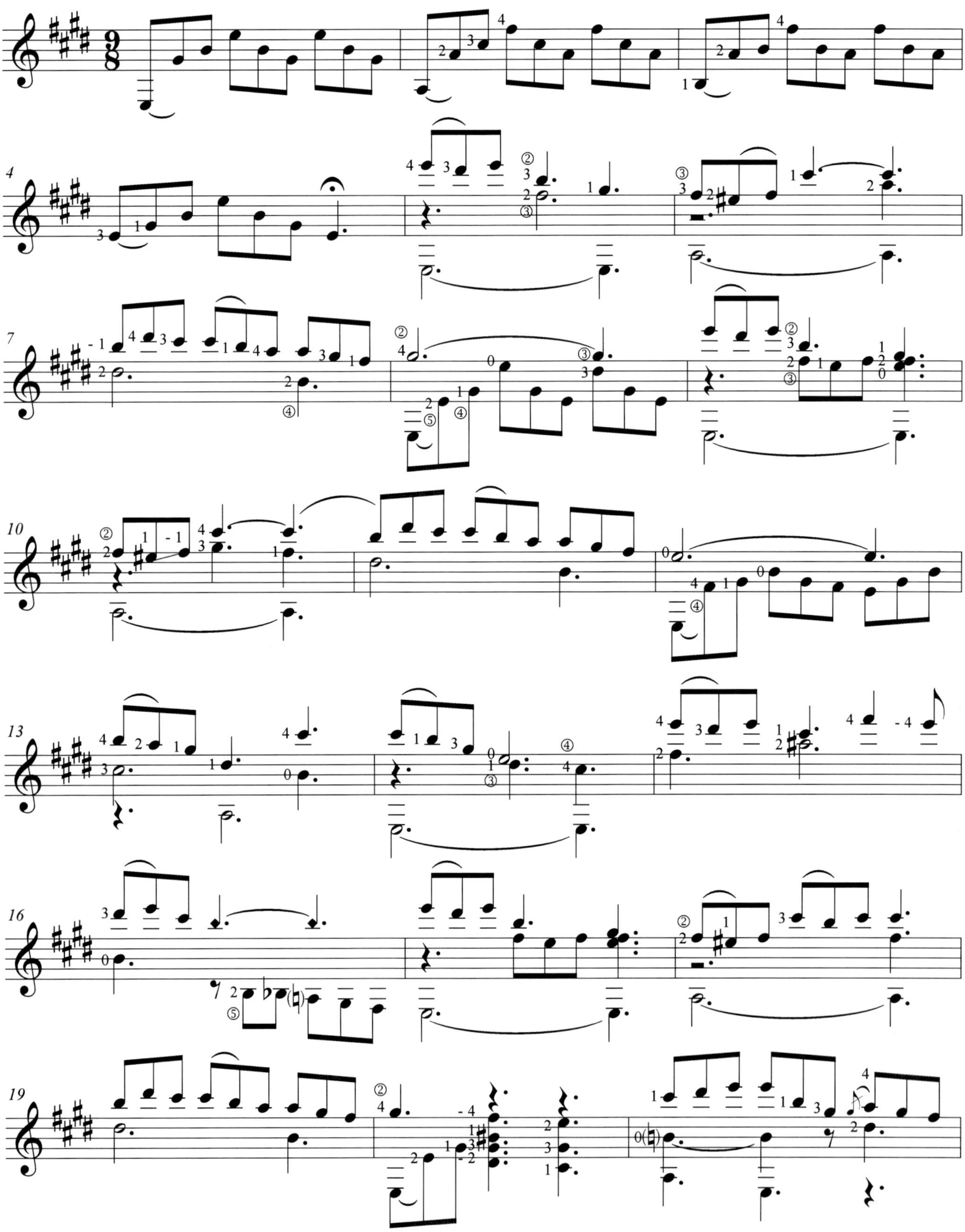

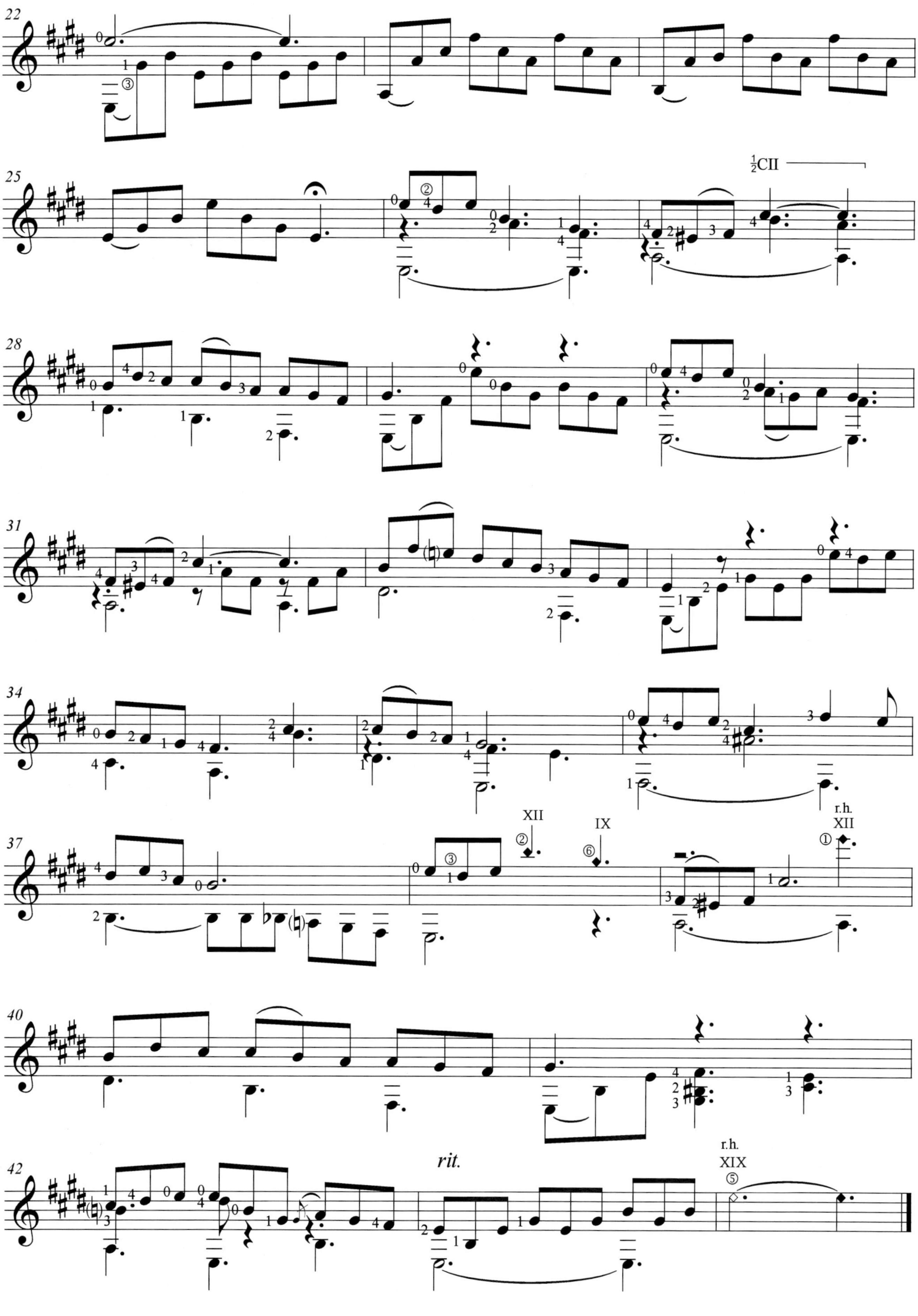
½CII
XII
IX
r.h.
XII
rit.
r.h.
XIX

Mighty Lak' a Rose

Ethelbert Nevin
(1862-1901)
arr. Tanja Mirić

Freely ♩ = 72

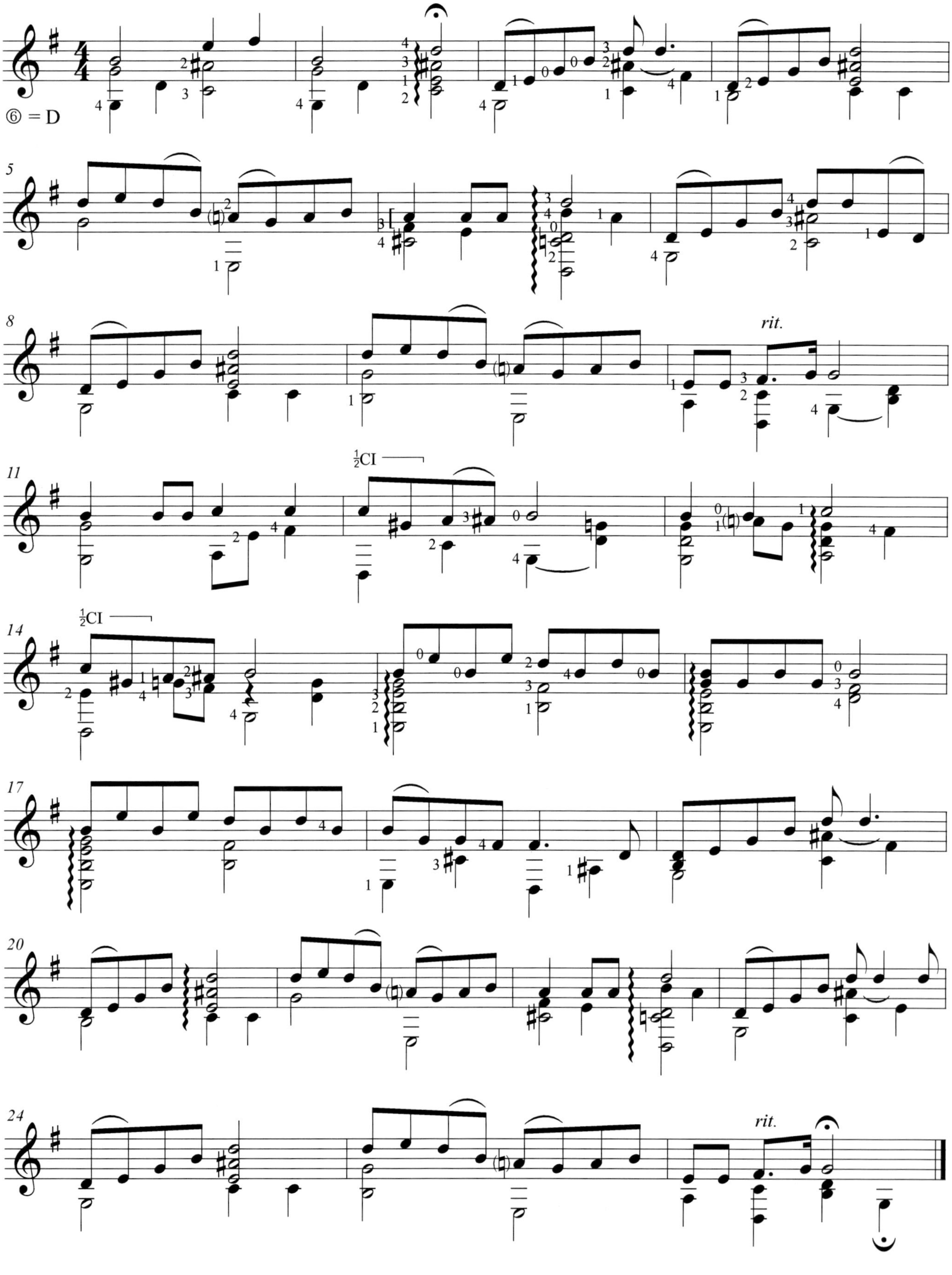

Aura Lee

George R. Poulton
(1828-1867)
arr. Tanja Mirić

Andante ♩ = 82

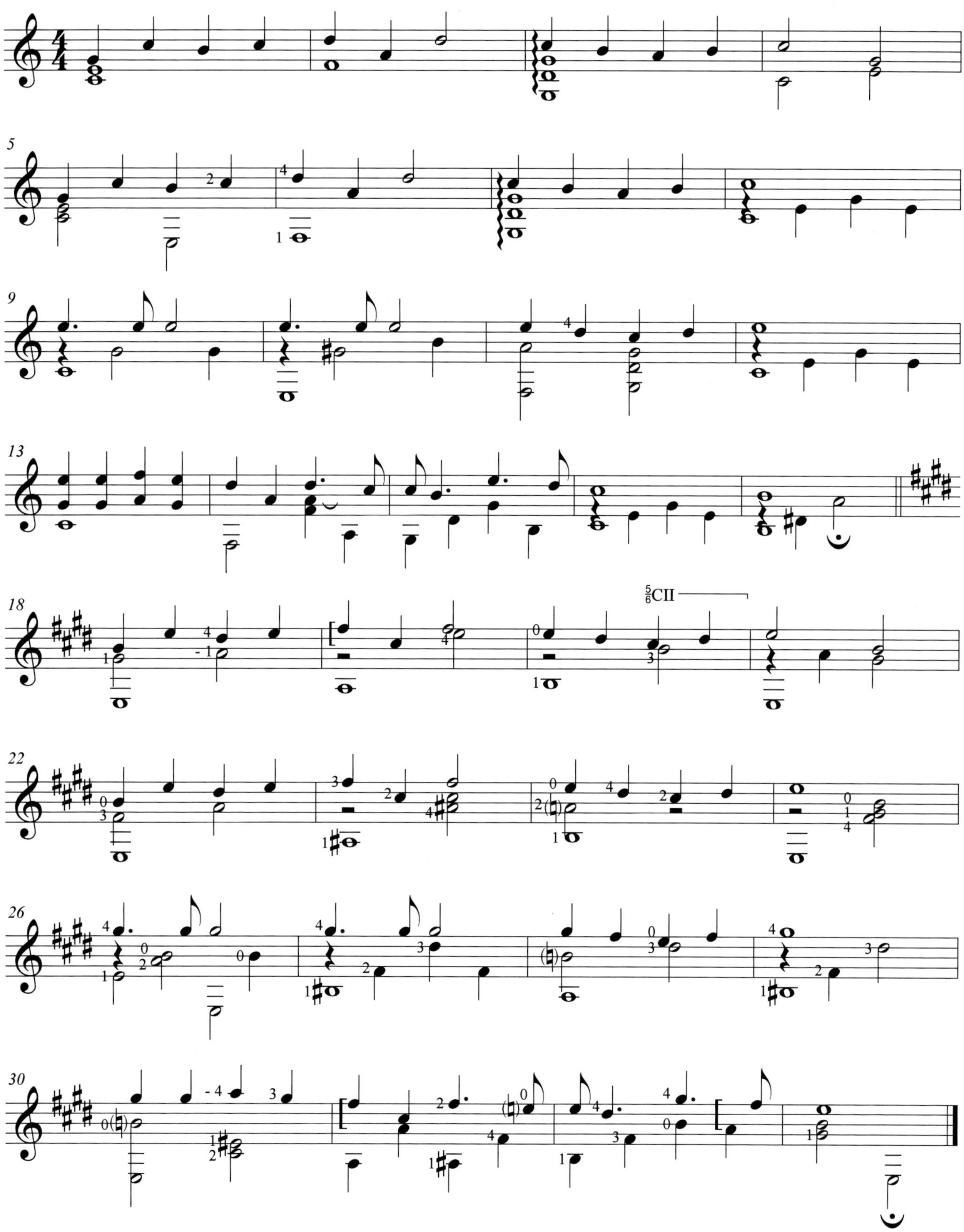

To a Wild Rose
Op. 51 No. 1 from "Woodland Sketches"

Edward MacDowell
(1860-1908)
arr. Tanja Mirić

Tenderly ♩ = 55

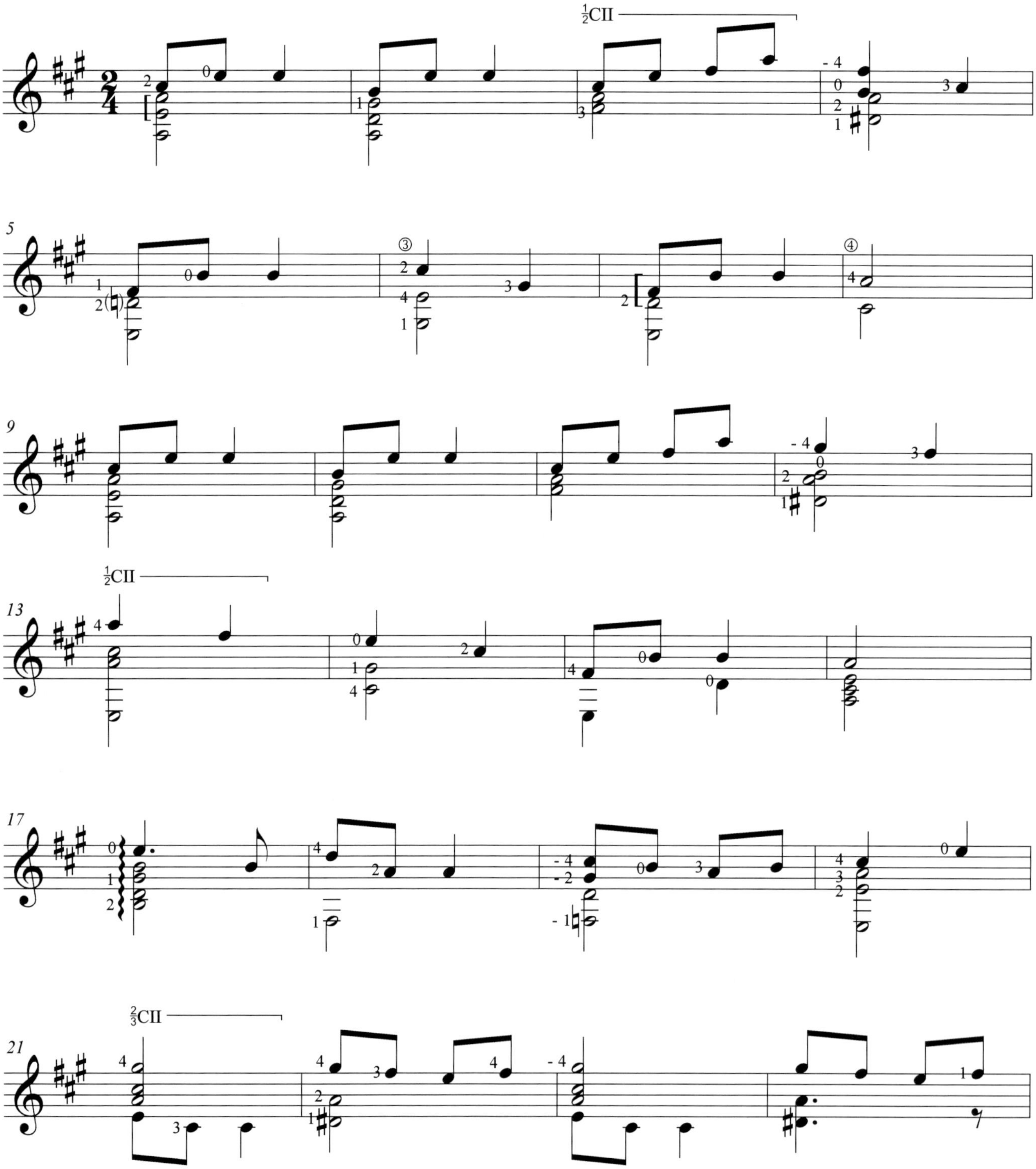

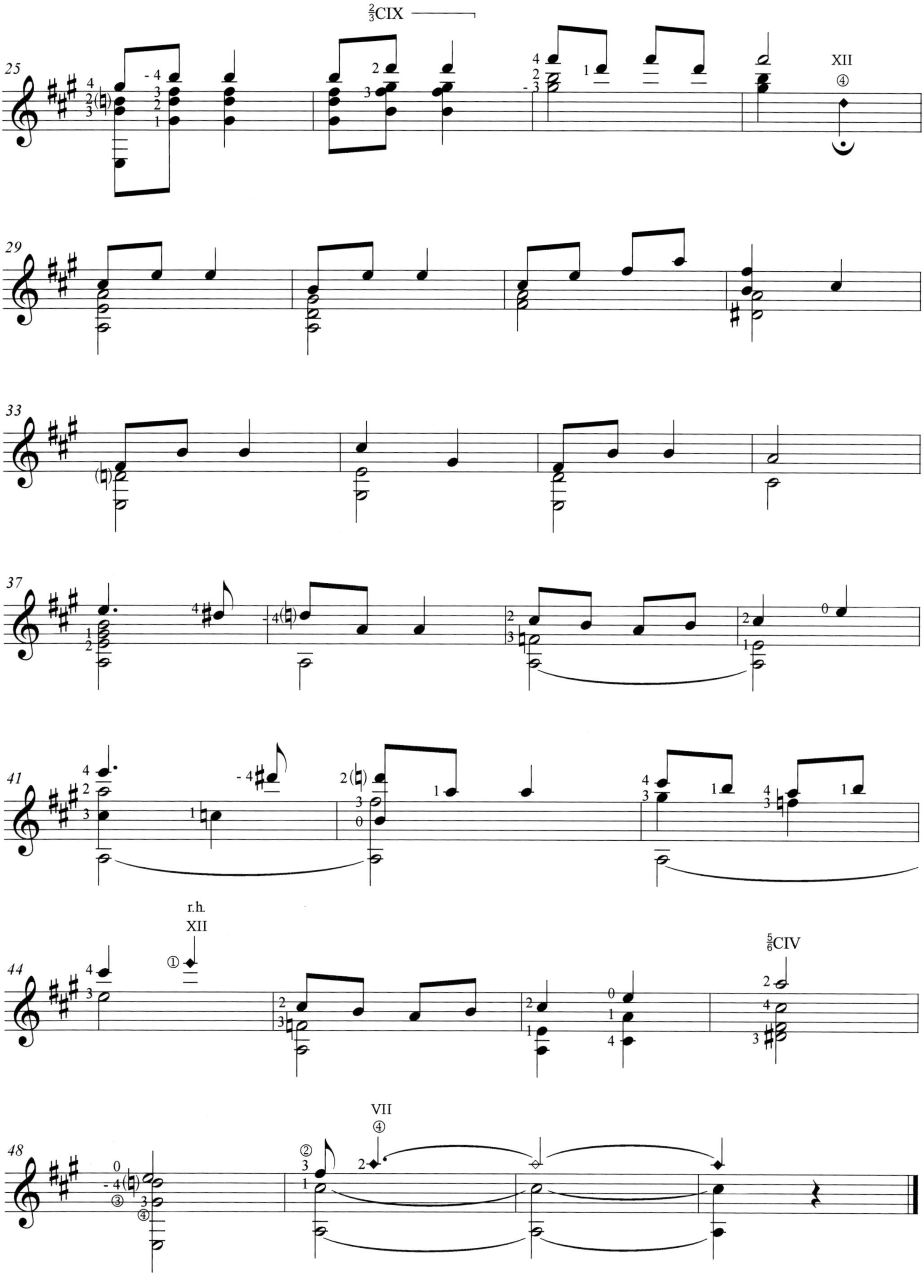

2/3CIX
XII
r.h.
XII
5/6CIV
VII

Johnny Has Gone for a Soldier

Civil War Ballad
arr. Tanja Mirić

Slowly ♩ = 76

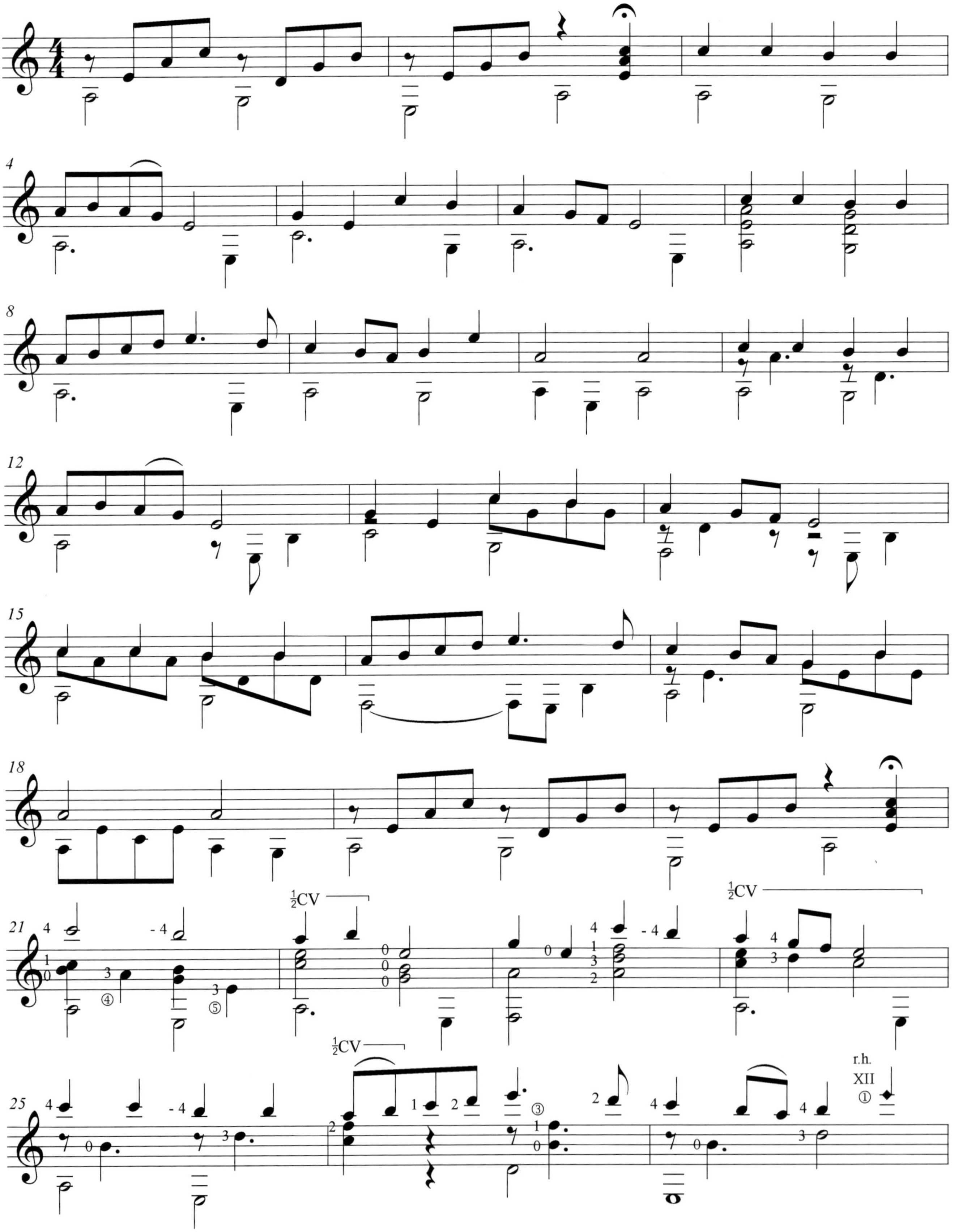

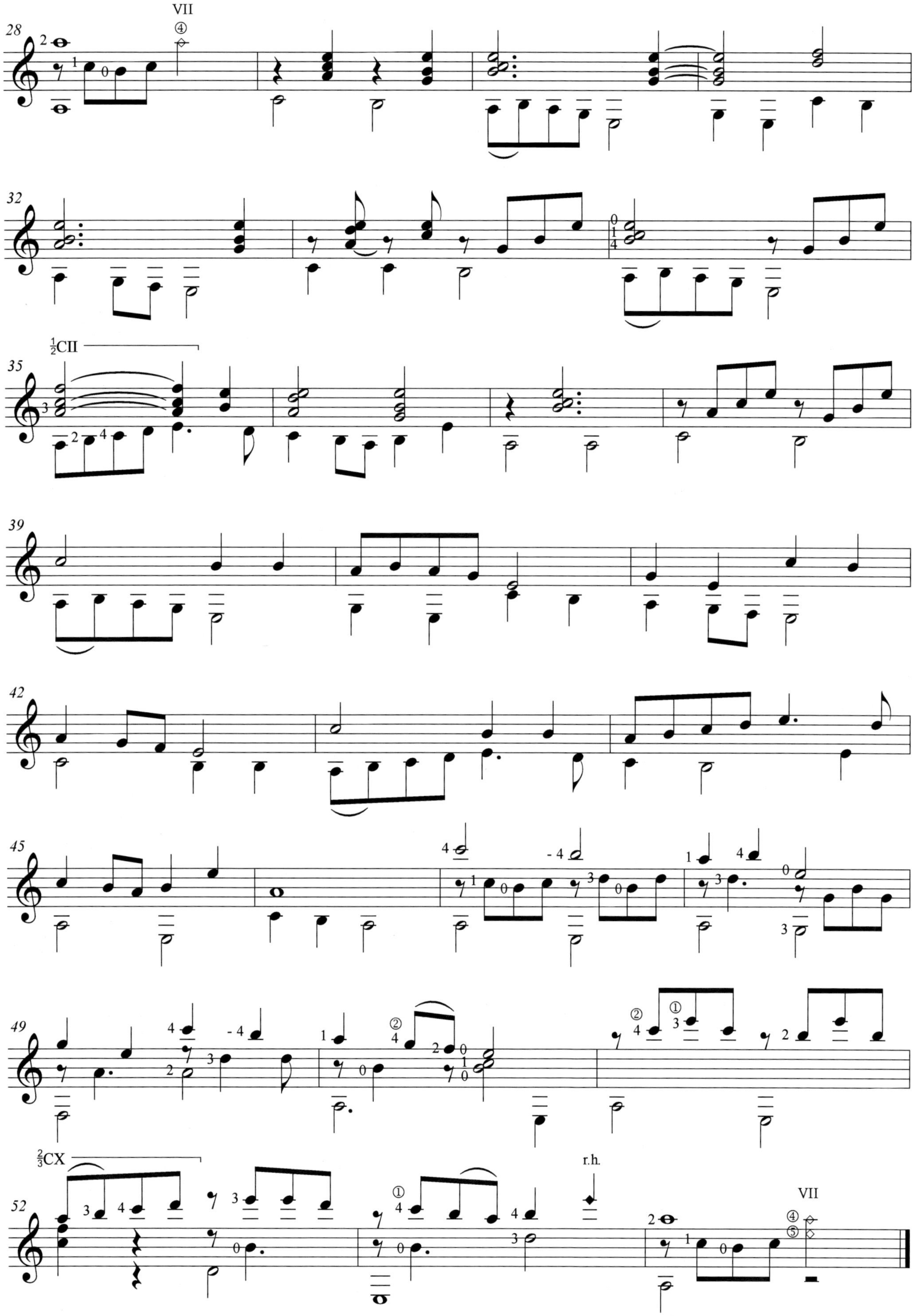
VII
½CII
⅔CX
r.h.
VII

Shady Grove

Appalachian folk song
arr. Tanja Mirić

Andante ♩ = 80

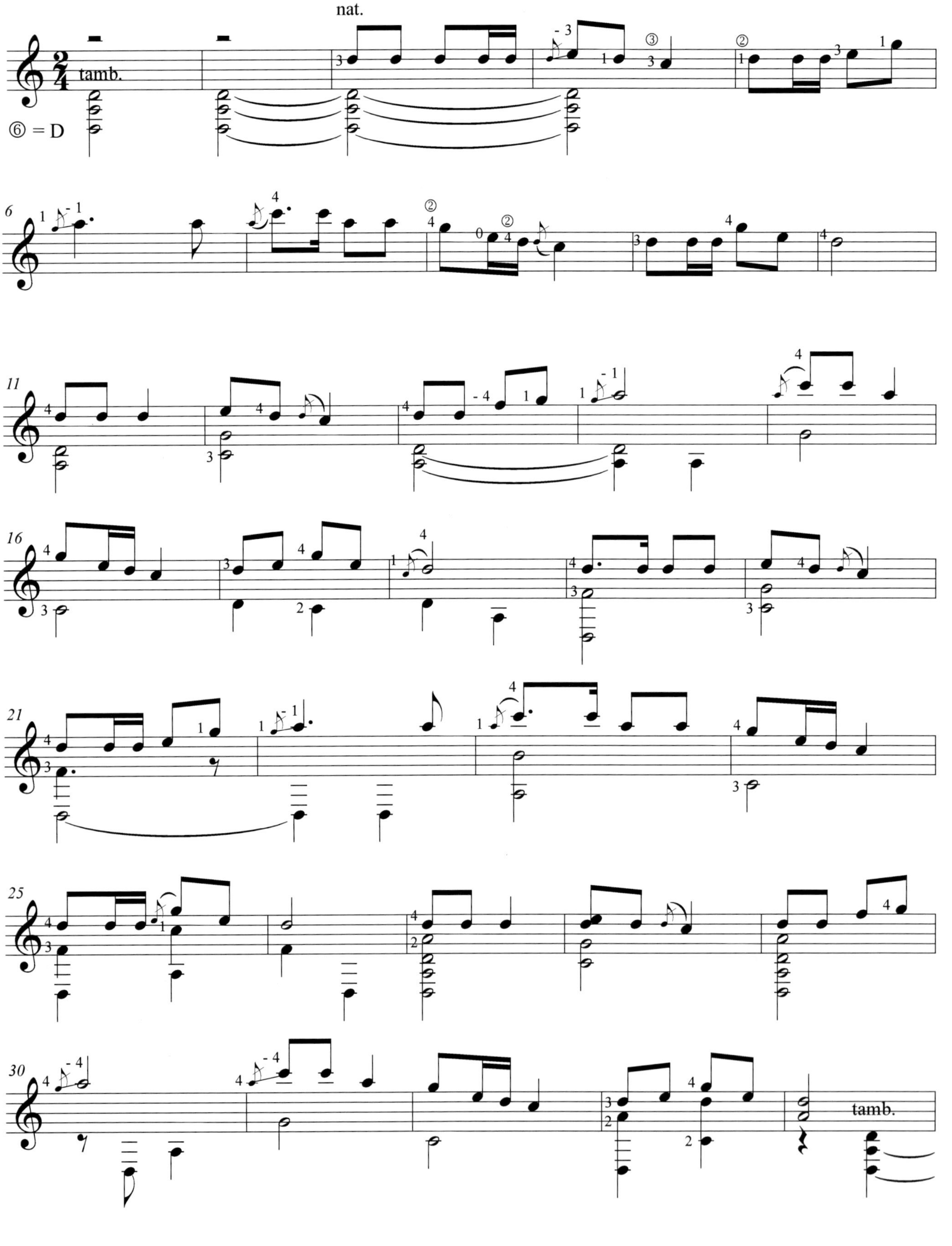

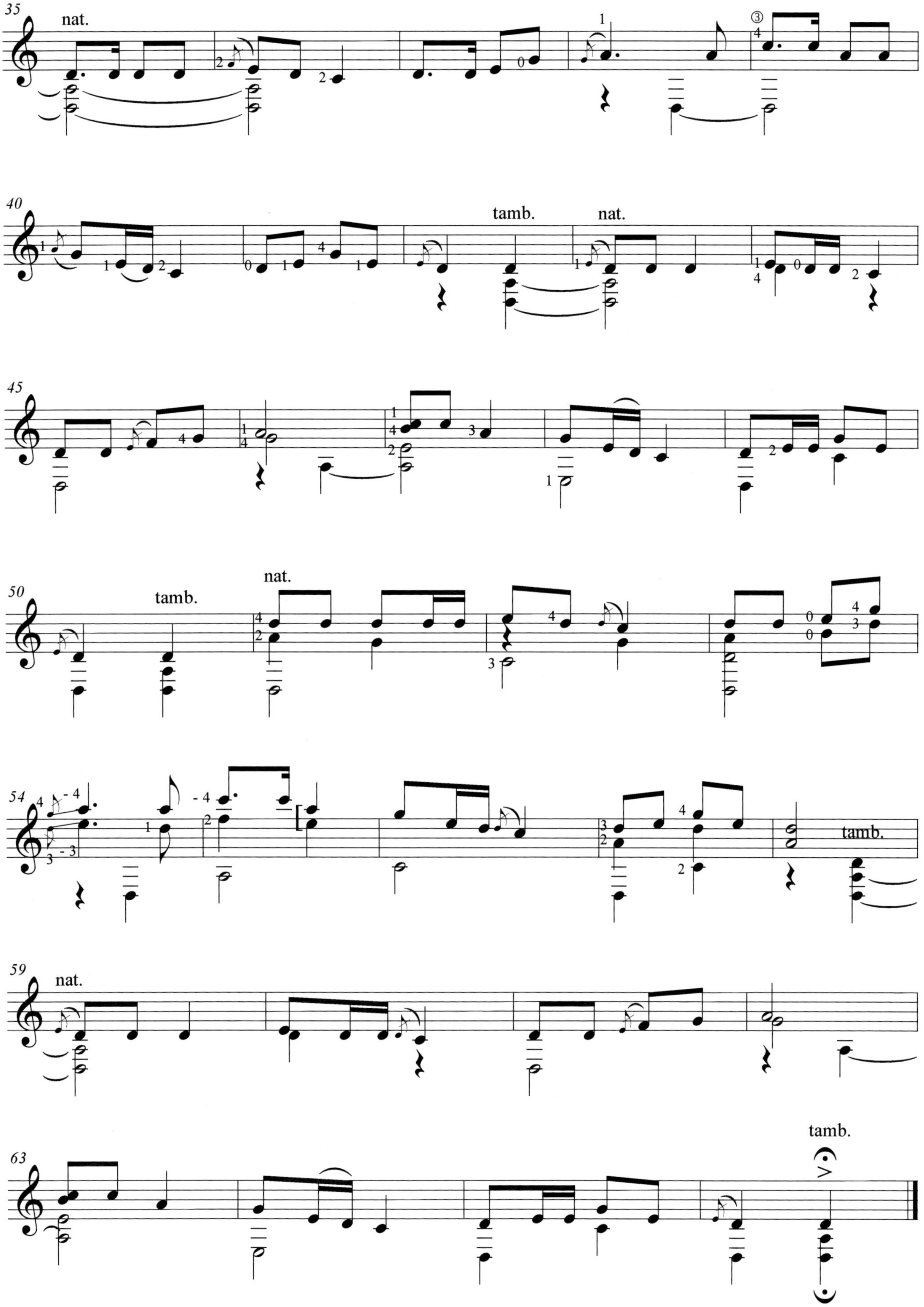
nat.
tamb.
nat.
tamb.
nat.
tamb.
nat.
tamb.

Land of Rest

Early American Sacred Melody
arr. Tanja Mirić

Flowing ♩ = 116

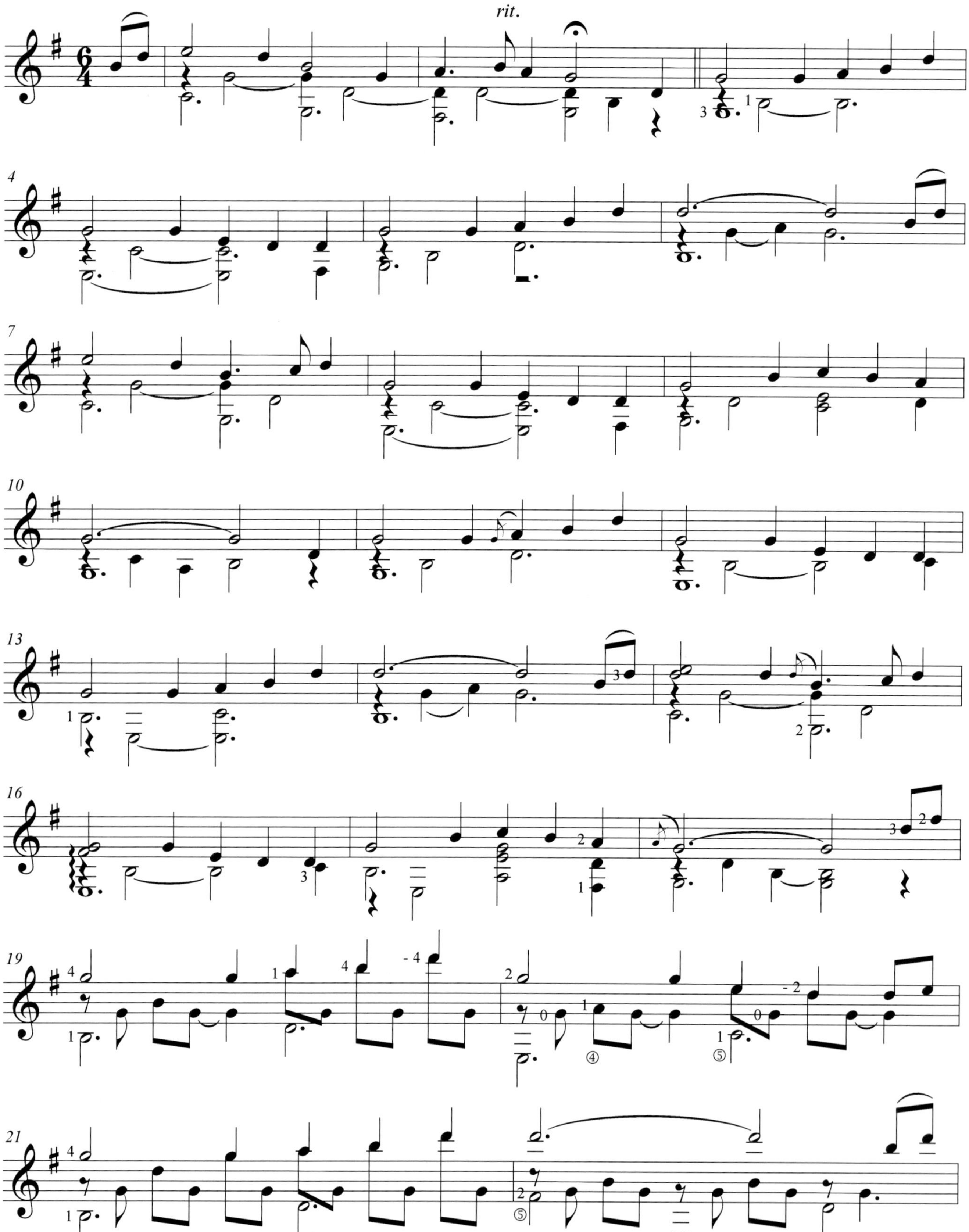

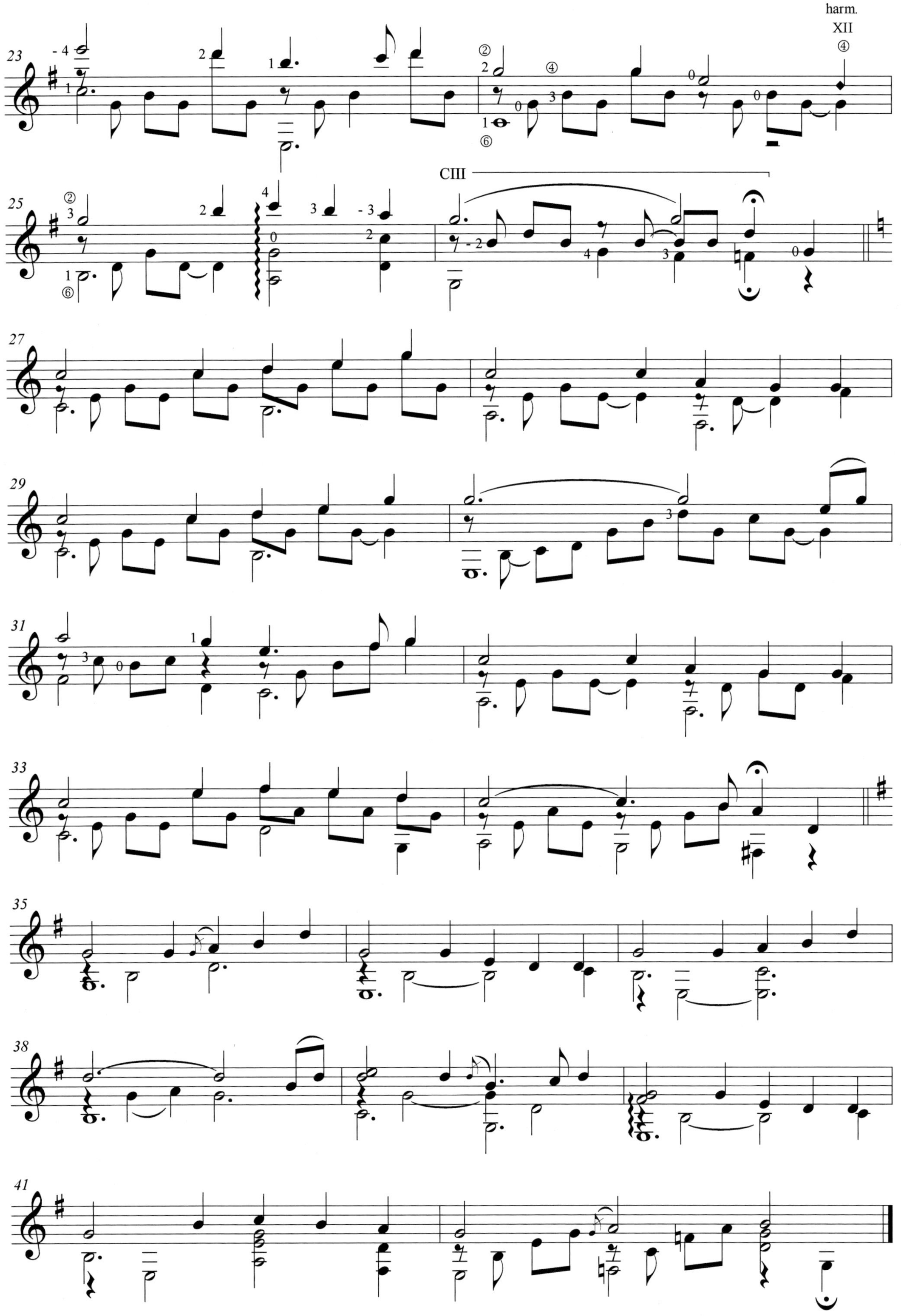
harm.
XII
CIII

Other Mel Bay Classical Guitar Solo Collections

6 Neapolitan Songs for Solo Classic Guitar (Scheldt)
A Dozen Italian Diversions for Guitar Solo (DiBenedetti)
Airs and Ballads for Classic Guitar (Lehmann-Haupt)
Arias for Acoustic Guitar: Operatic Melodies for Solo Guitar (Edwards)
Ashokan Farewell Guitar Arrangement (Ungar/Lehmann-Haupt)
Balkan Melodies for Classic Guitar Solo (Mirić)
Christmas Songs for Classical Guitar (Castle)
Ciclos: Music of the Sephardic Jews for Classic Guitar (Akiva)
Civil War Suite for Classical Guitar (Brew)
Classical and Flamenco Guitar Solos and Etudes (Elysa Hochman/Jason Hochman)
Classical Guitar Tunes - Fun Solos to Play (Calmes)
Classic Guitar Tunes - Gospel Favorites (Calmes)
Classic Tangos (Halen)
Complete Works of Scott Joplin: 52 PIano Rags, Waltzes & Marches Transcribed for Guitar Solo (De Chiaro)
Contemporary Irish Music for Classic Guitar Solo (Feeley)
Devotion: Sacred Solos for Guitar (W. Bay)
Favorite Hymns for Classical Guitar (Castle)
Five Popular Persian Ballads for Solo Guitar (Afshar)
Five Women Composers Arranged for Guitar (Newman)
Folk songs and Dances of the Jewish People for Acoustic Guitar (Back)
Early American Hymn Favorites for Classical Guitar (Mirić)
Great American Marches, Polkas & Grand Concert Waltzes for Acoustic Guitar (Back)
Greek Traditional Music for Acoustic Guitar (Borjanic)
Irish Folk Songs for Classical Guitar (Marsh)
Melodies of the Far East for Guitar (Tuan Vu)
Nineteen Gilbert & Sullivan Favorites Arranged for Classical Guitar (Marrington)
O'Carolan Favorites for Classic Guitar (Böger)
Romantic Arias for Classical Guitar (Eckels)
Russian Folk Songs for Guitar Solo (Borjanic)
Solo Guitar Hymnal: Classic Guitar Solos for the Liturgical Calendar Year (Bass)
Stephen Foster for Classic Guitar (Böger)
The Christmas Book - Carols Arrangeds for Acoustic Guitar (Barreiro)
The Holiday Gig Book (Johnstone)
Traditional Christmas Favorites for Classical Guitar (Siktberg)
Turlough O'Carolan Irish Harp Pieces for Classic Guitar (Böger)
Wedding Favorites for Classical Guitar (De Chiaro)

Progressive Cello Solos

Beginning Level

Christine Watts

WWW.MELBAY.COM

Welcome teachers and students!

Since beginning cello repertoire has always seemed limited, I wrote this book to introduce delightful, engaging new music to the novice cellist. With educational and fun pieces to learn and enjoy, it's easier to instill a solid technical foundation and form a constructive attitude about practice.

By design, the entire book is in first position, and the melodies are in progressive order of difficulty. It contains many pieces that are inspired by or about animals which have universal appeal, and many great recital pieces both long and short all with piano accompaniments.

New techniques are introduced and explained throughout the book followed by illustrative pieces using them.

Examples:

- Second finger for C on the A string and F on the D string
- The slur and how to play one
- Dotted notes, the tie and how to count them
- Stretch (extended) position both for flats and sharps
- Suggestions about how to use your bow for a better, more musical sound

Because it contains lively, educational, and inspiring pieces, this book used in conjunction with your basic method book will satisfy all the needs of your beginning students. It will also enhance your teaching and provide new music for you to listen to and enjoy.

Christine Watts

Table of Contents

To make your notes sound more beautiful, use your entire bow on the ½ notes and most of it on the ¼ notes.

The Bee

Allegretto

German Folk Song

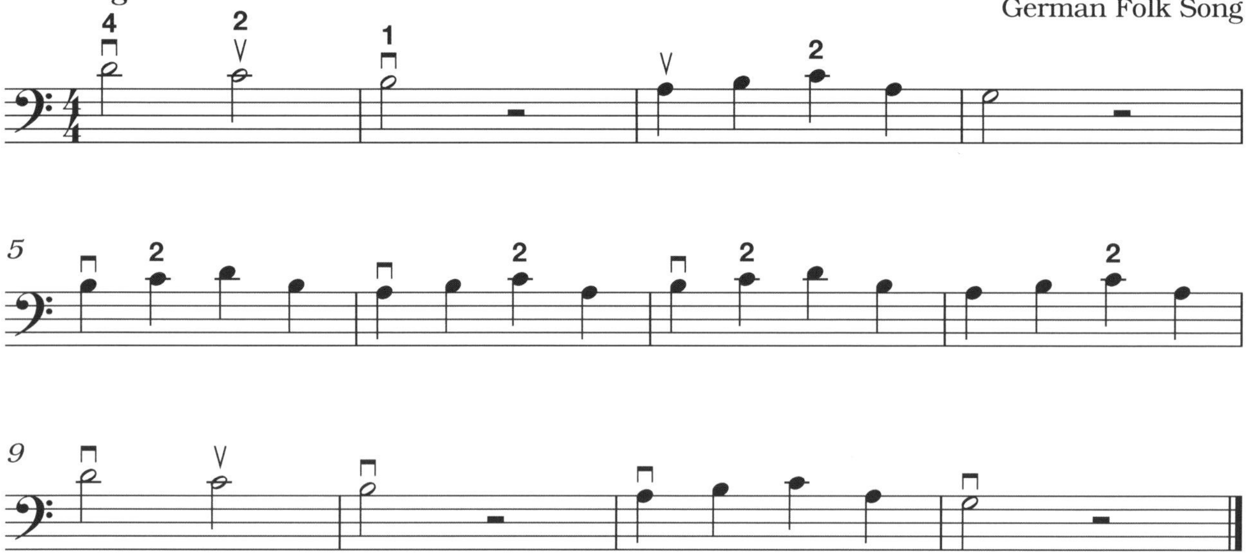

Because there are no C♯'s in *The Hobby Horse* or *The Bee*, use your 2nd finger on the A string for C instead of your 3rd which is for C♯.

The Hobby Horse

Allegretto

German Folk Song

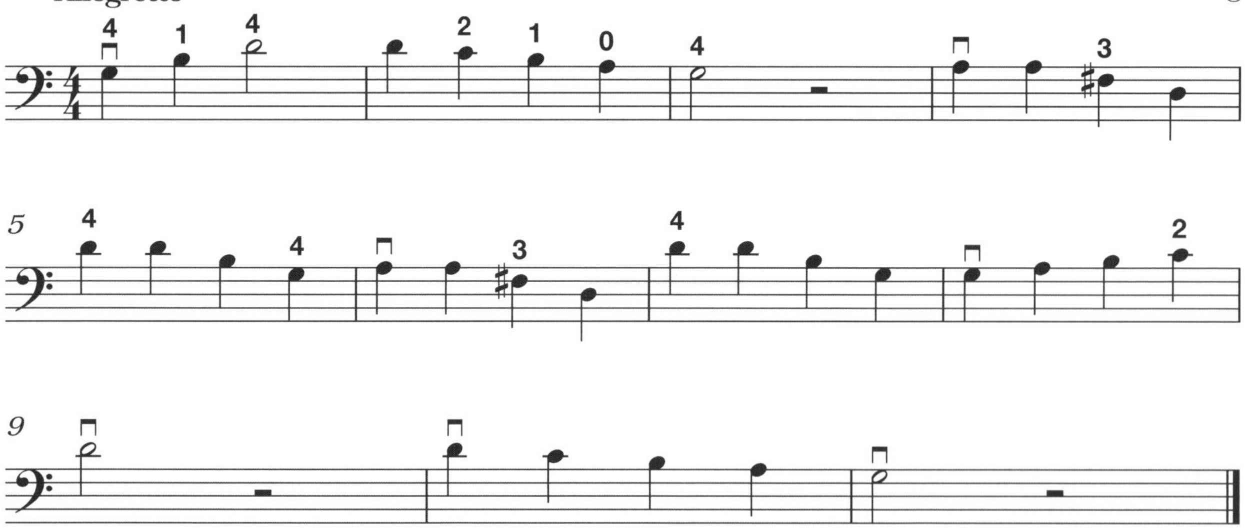

Elephants

Christine Watts

Pesante

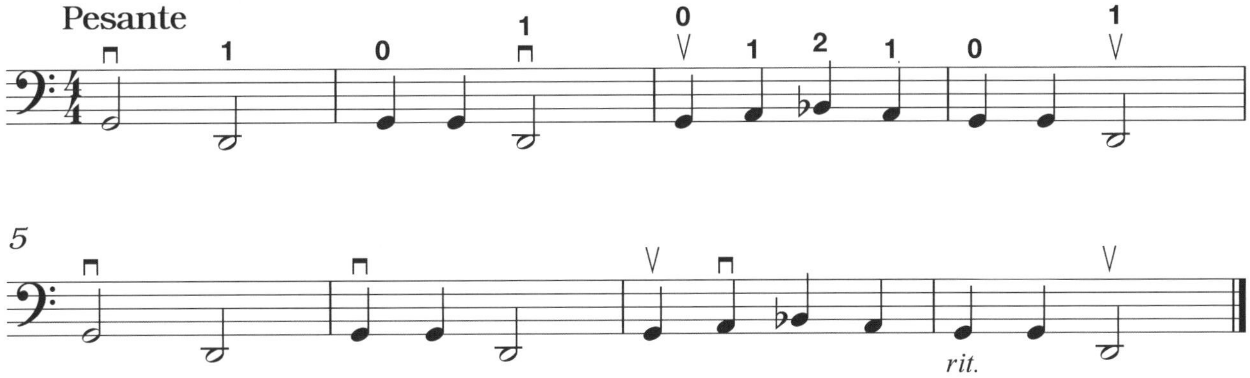

A dotted half note is 3 beats. A dot next to a note means add ½ the value of that note to itself. ½ the value of a half note is 1, so 2 + 1 = 3 beats for a dotted half note.

Willie & Tillie

Dolce

American Folk Song

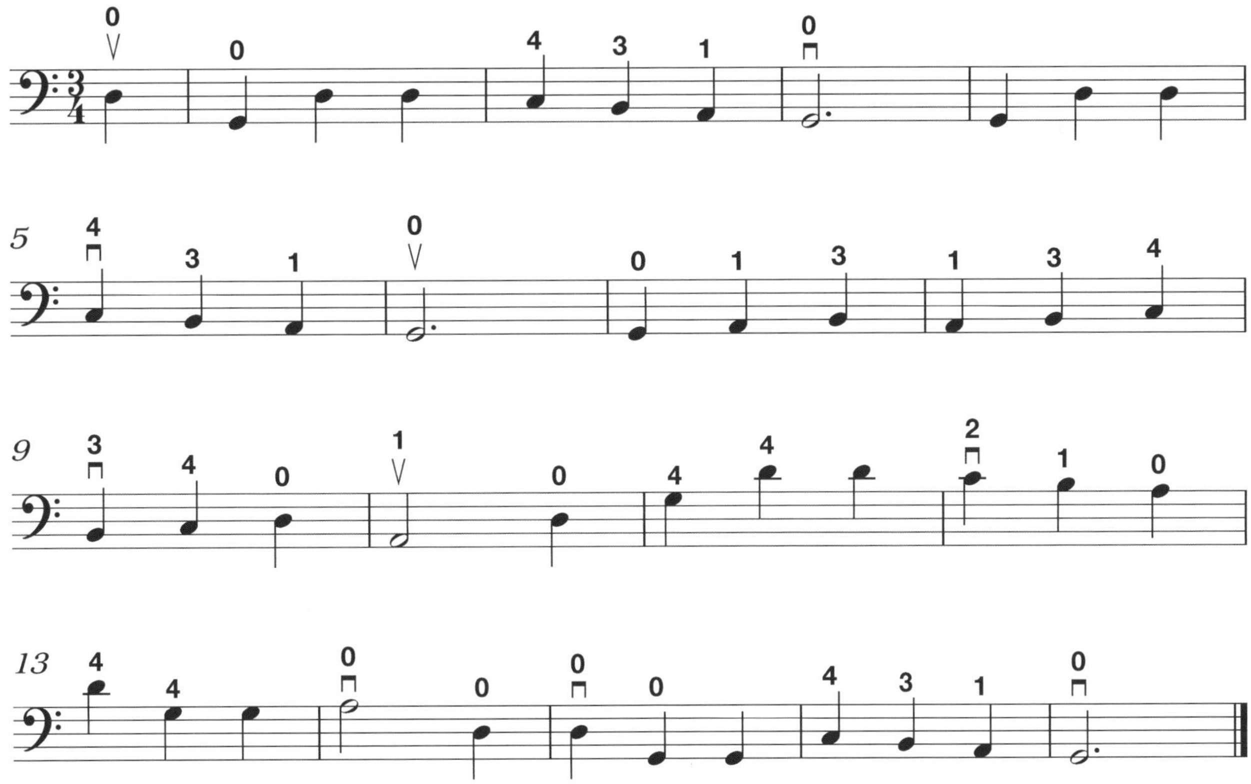

The Cuckoo

FOCUS: Move your bow very fast on the one-beat down bow so you'll have plenty of bow for the two-beat up bow.

Animato

English Folk Song

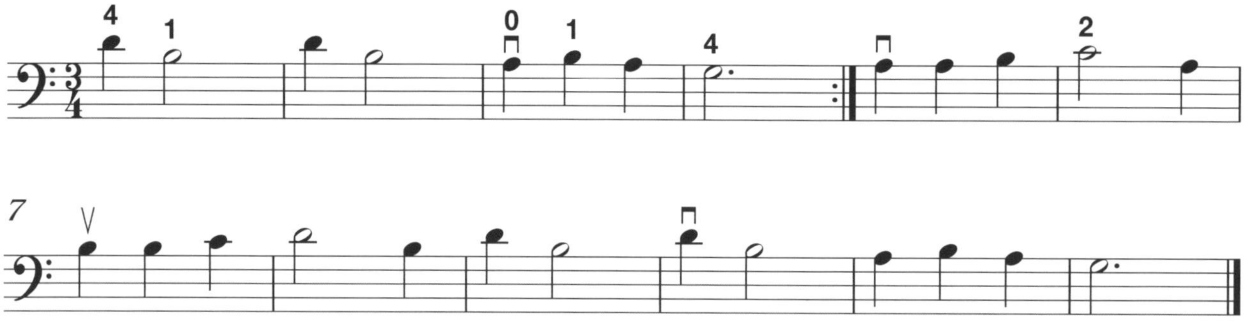

Monkeys Swinging in the Trees

Grazioso con moto

Christine Watts

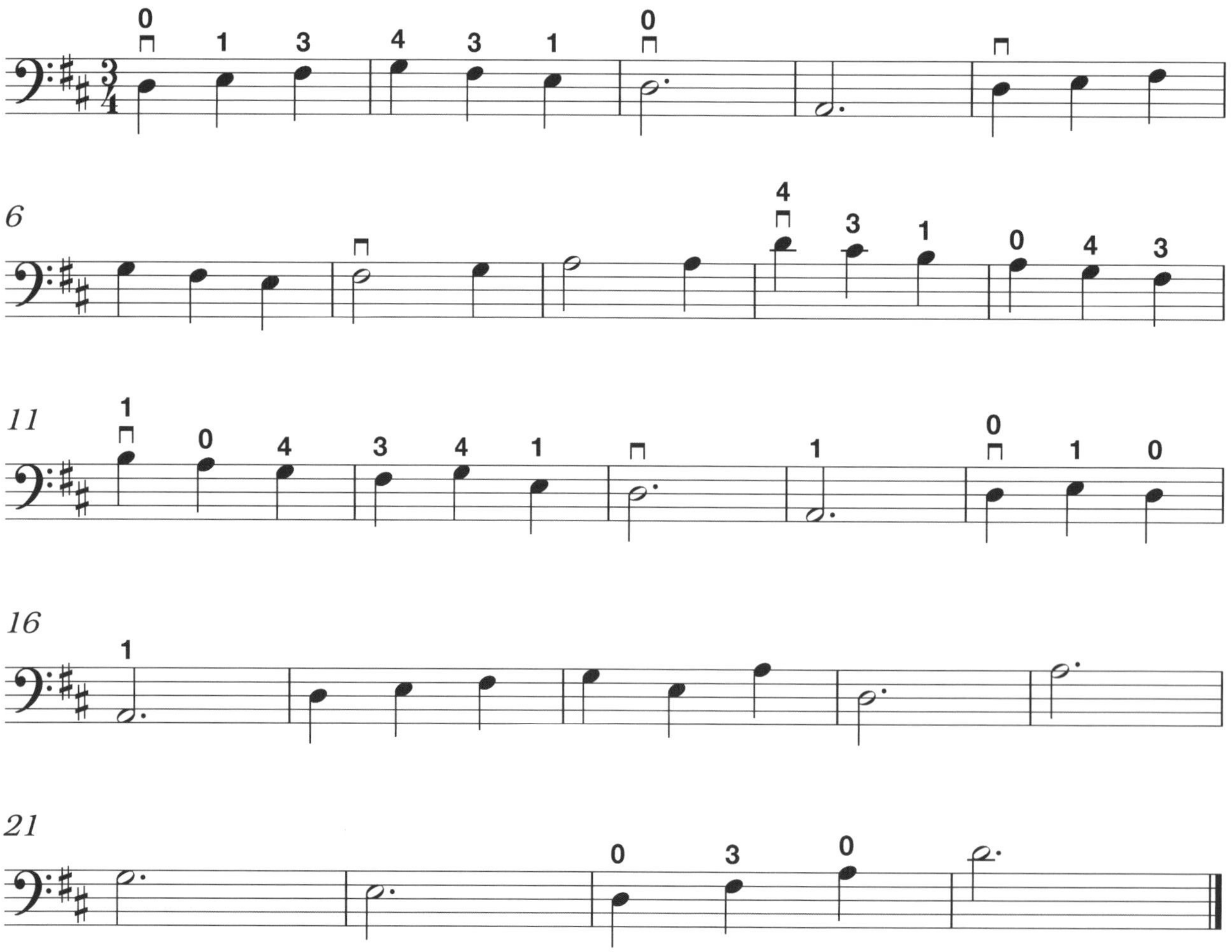

Eighth notes don't always require you to play fast. When you play Ladybugs, use your whole bow on the slurs, and most of it on the single notes. This will make your notes sound more beautiful.

Ladybugs

Christine Watts

Allegro Animato

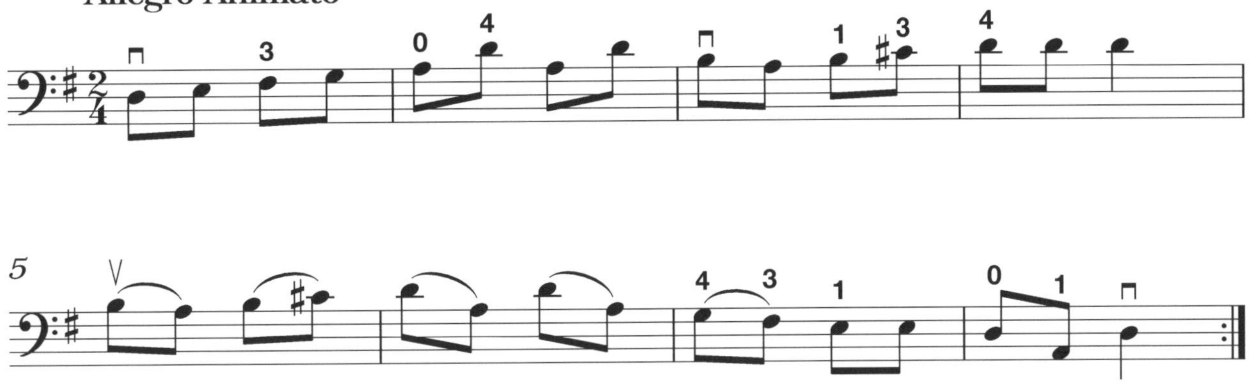

Ladybug Fly Away

American Folk Song

Allegretto con moto

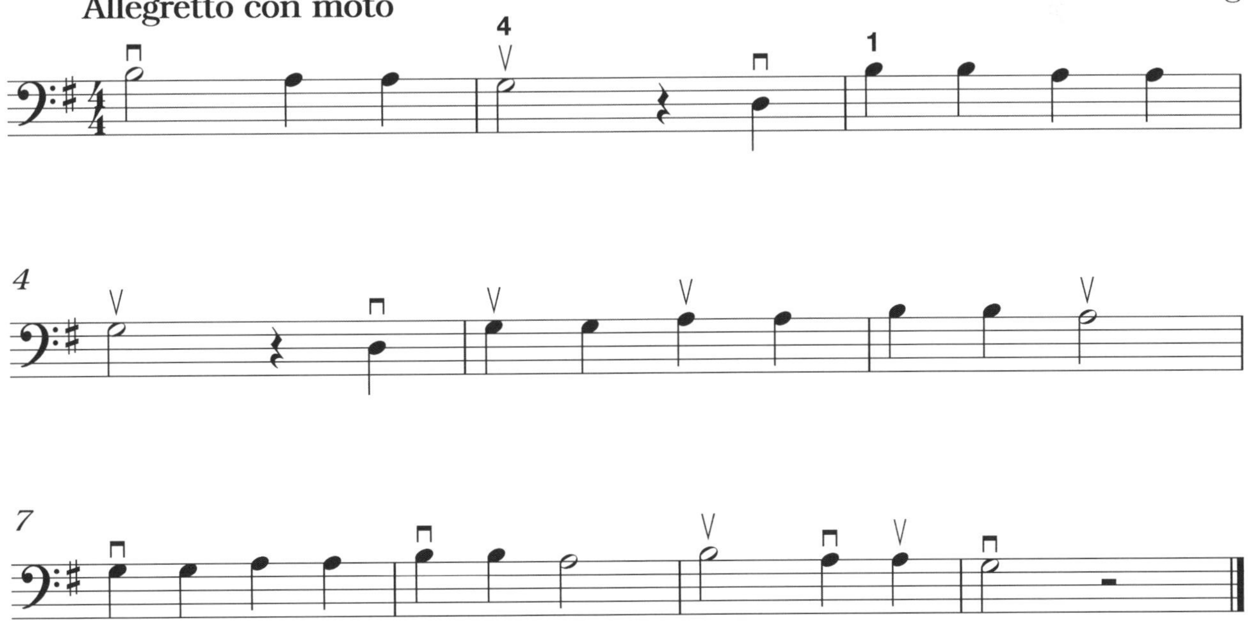

A slur is a curved line over two or more notes which connects them. After you play the first note, keep your bow moving in the same direction and play the others.

The Contented Cow

Christine Watts

Dolce con moto

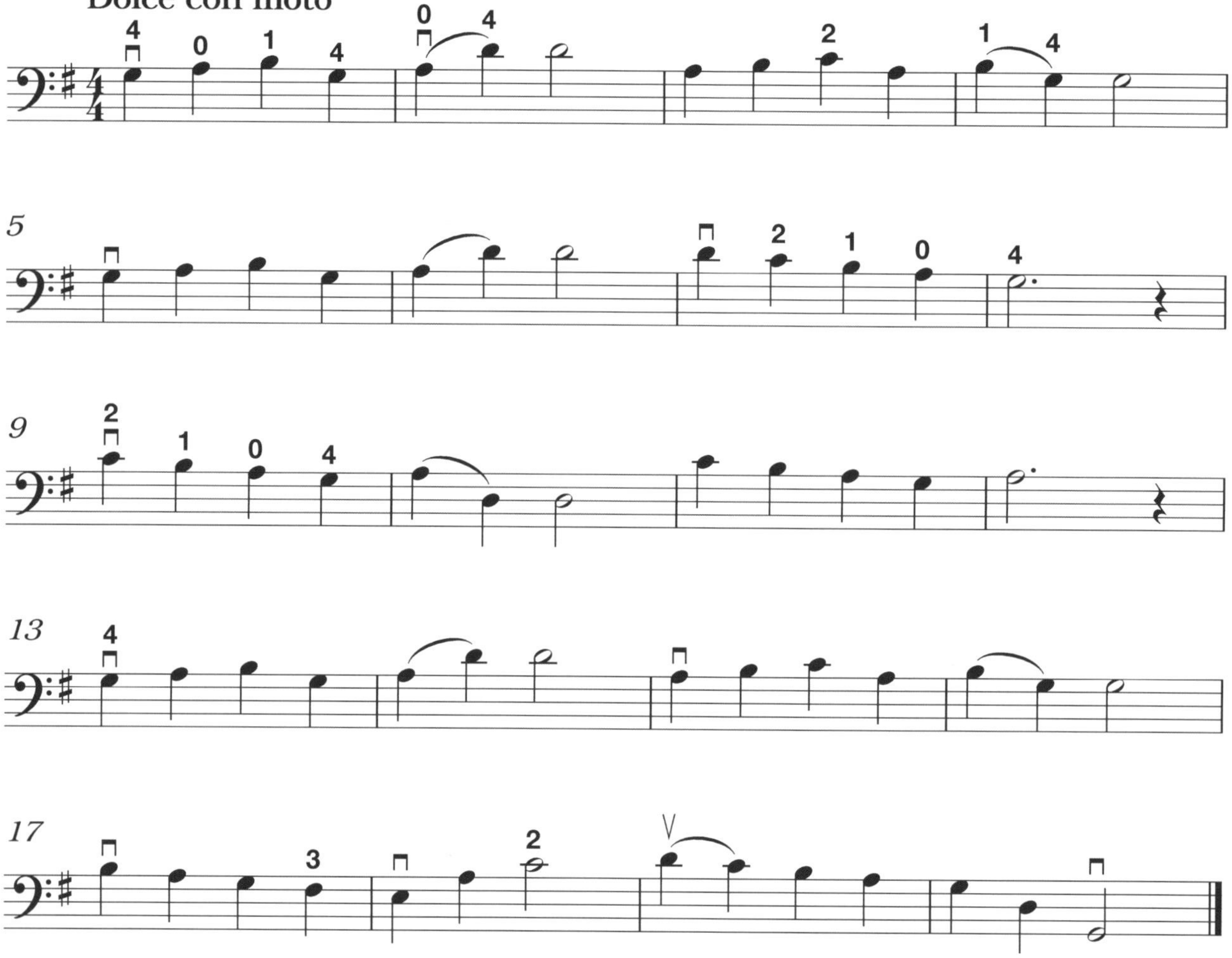

Slur Exercise

Use half your bow only on the first note and the other half on the second note. Play on all strings.

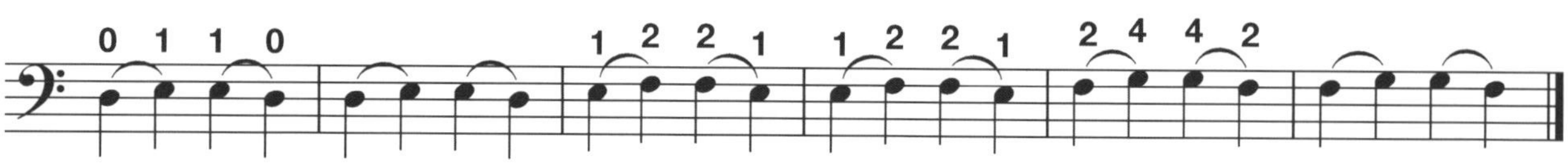

Since two notes slurred uses a lot of bow, move your bow fast on the single note to get back to where you started.

Country Dance

Beethoven

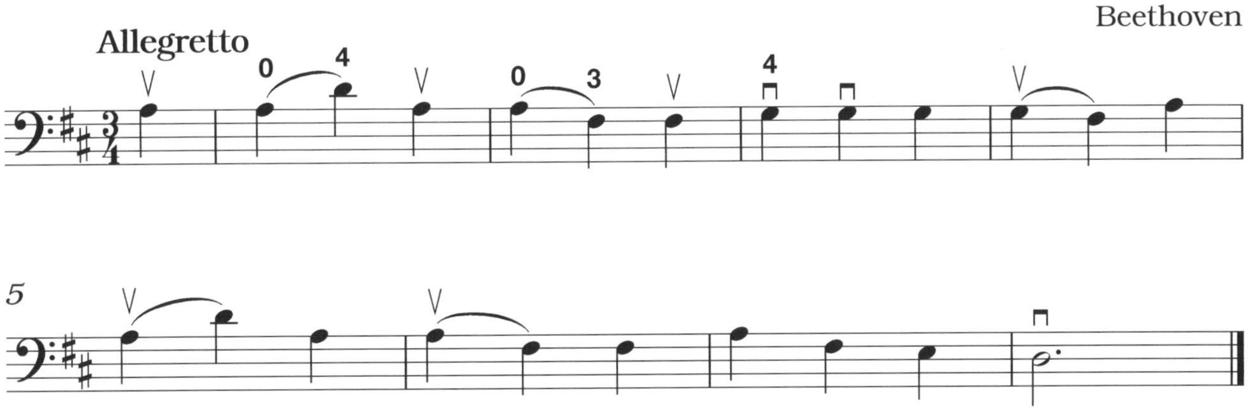

The Clever Fox

Polish Folk Song

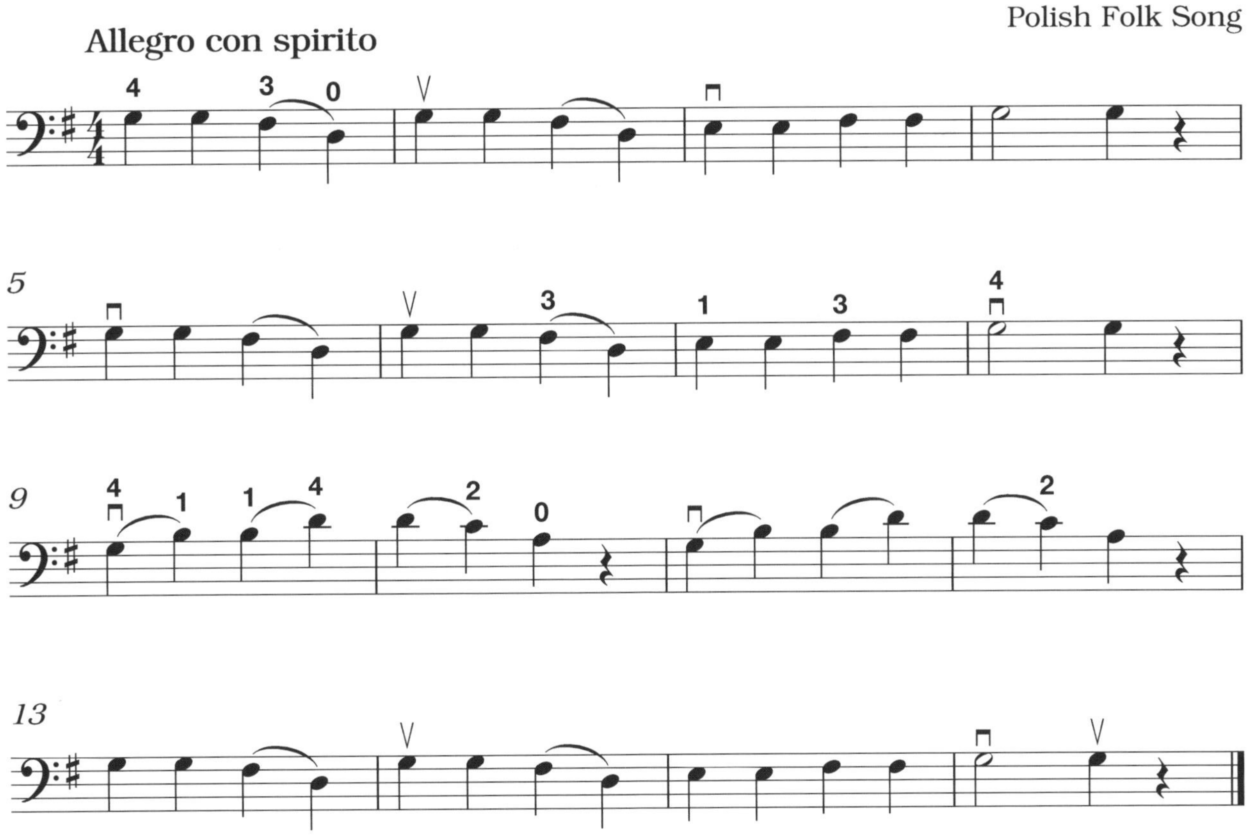

The Zebra's Dance

Christine Watts

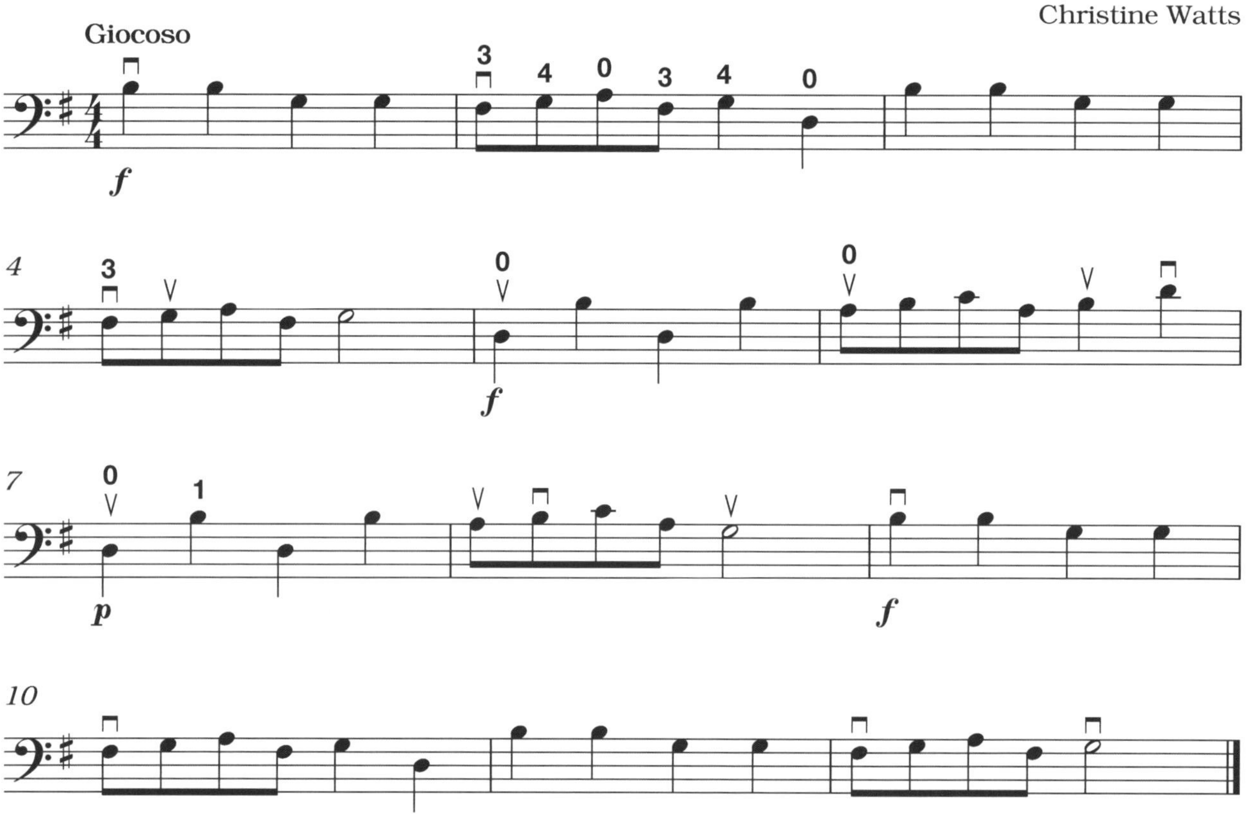

Lines and dots can have many meanings. Usually, a straight line over a note means to press a little harder on it. This can make a pulse or just emphasize the note.

Sister Come Dance With Me

American Folk Song

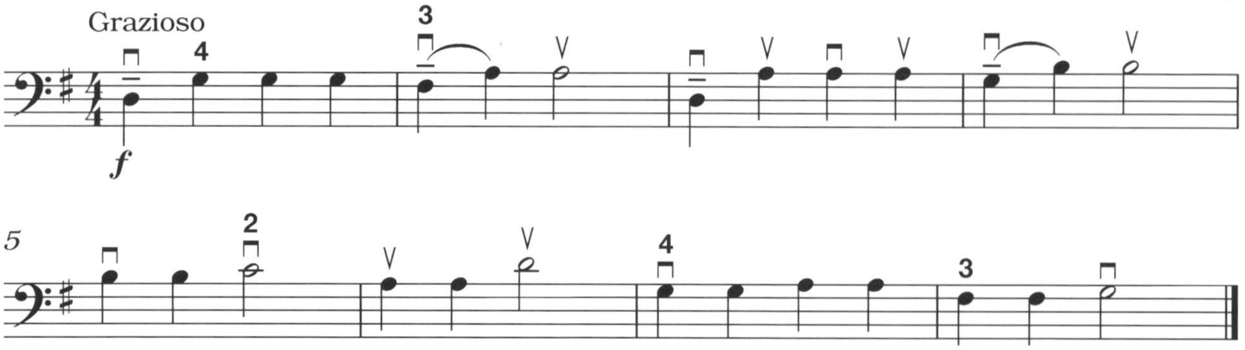

The Drum

William Duncombe

Tempo di marcia

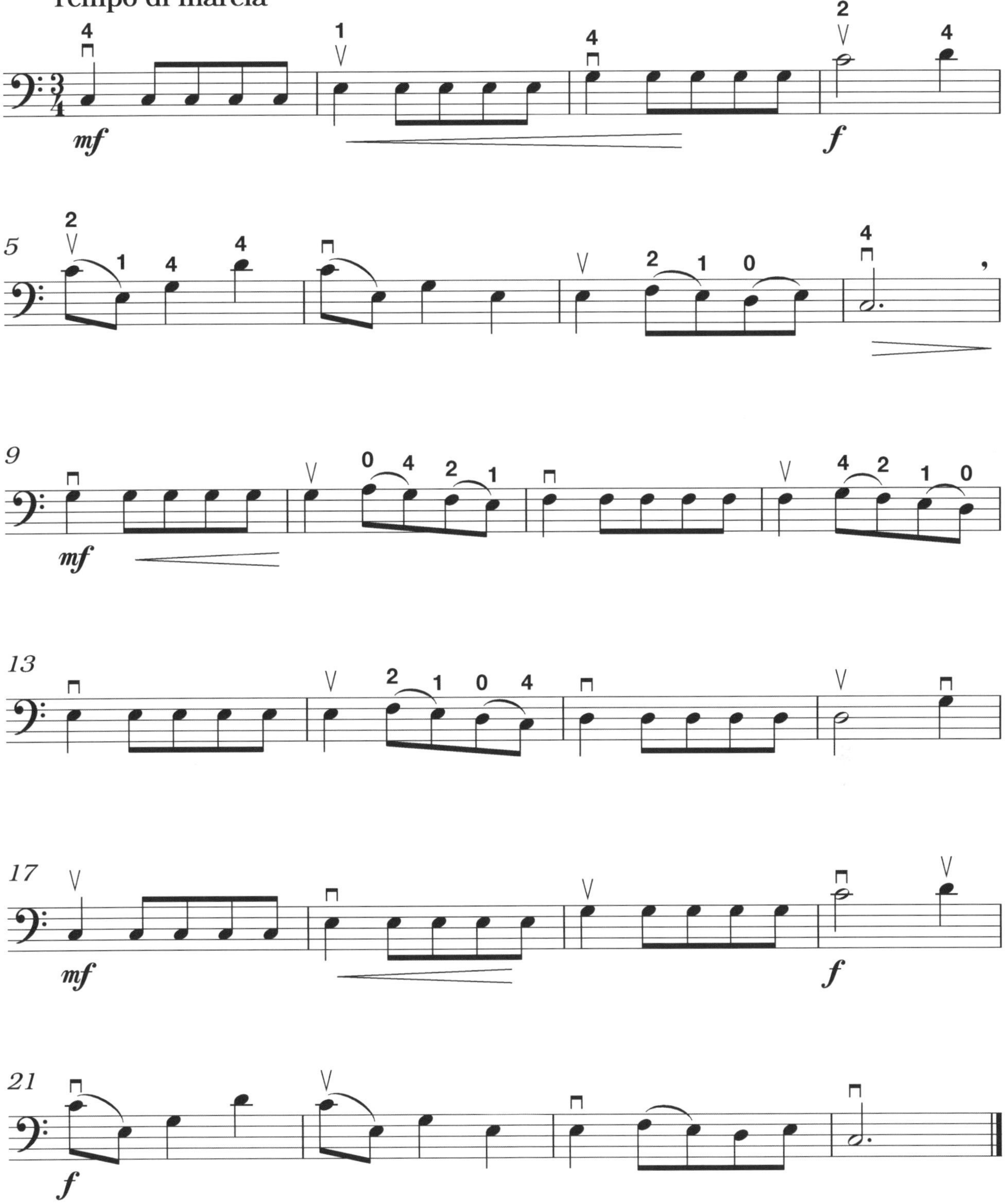

Laughing Song

("Die Fledermaus," Opera act II)

Johann Strauss II

Allegretto, Grazioso

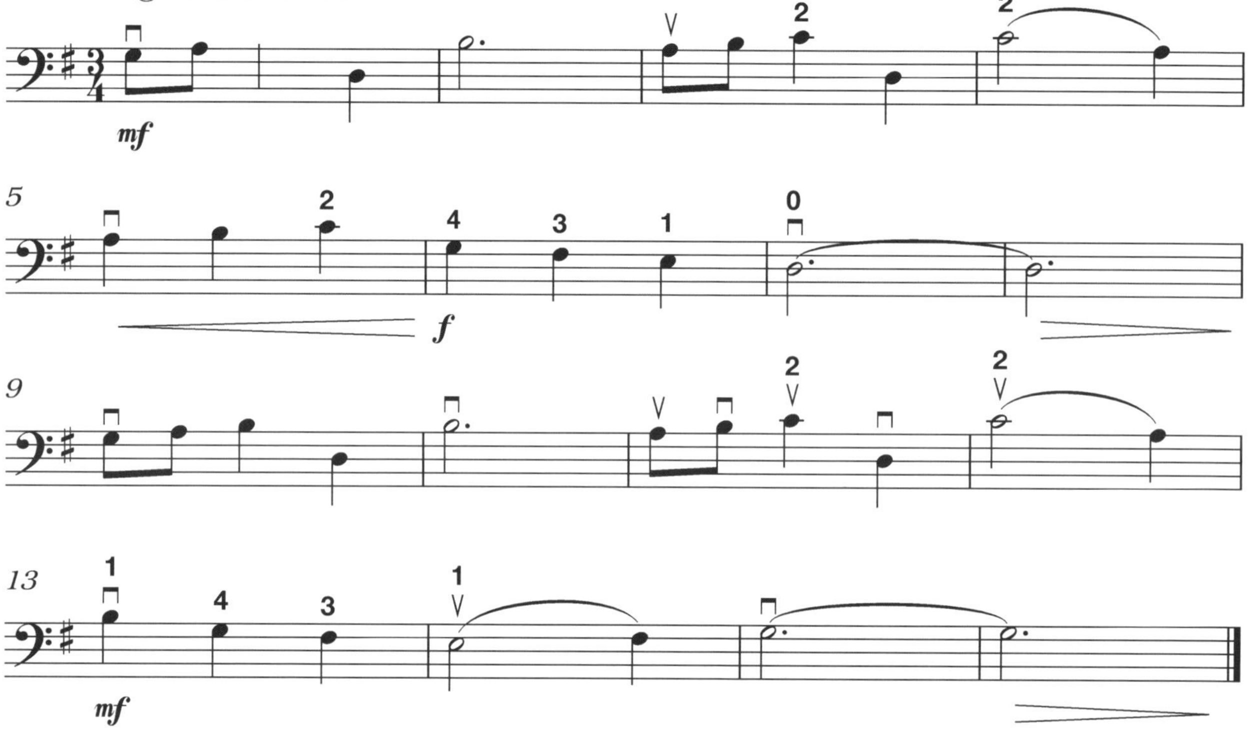

The Magic Ring

Dolce

Old Lithuanian Song

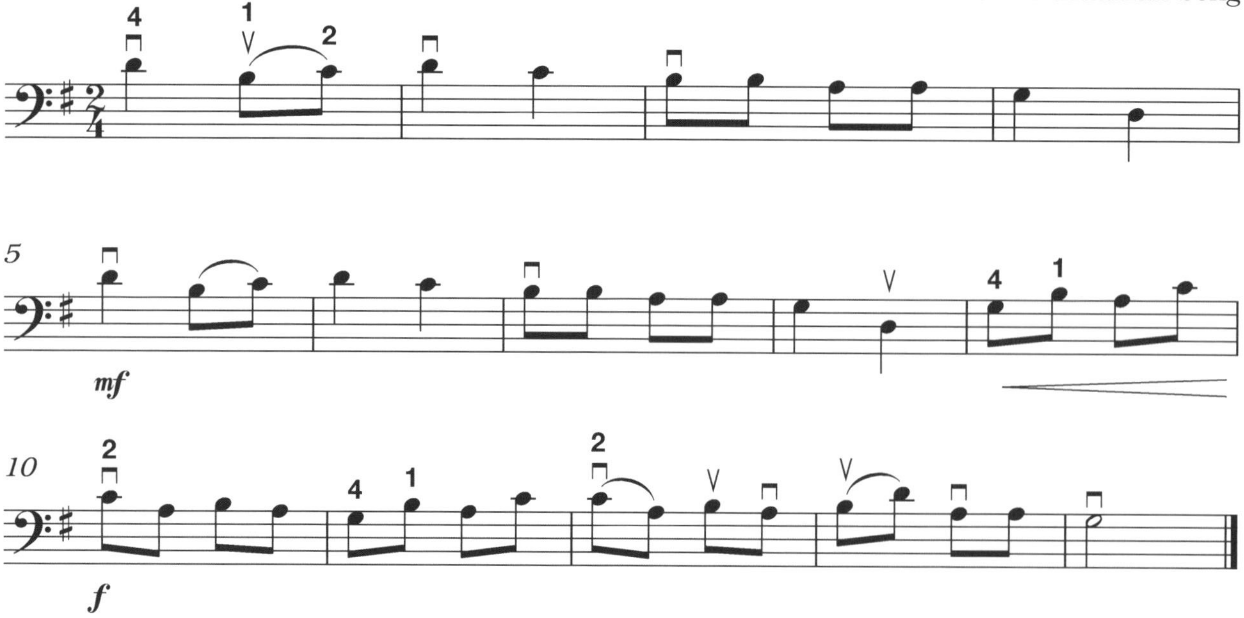

If you see dots over the notes in a slur, it means gently or abruptly stop your bow between them. This bowing is usually played up bow.

Minuet in G

Joseph Haydn

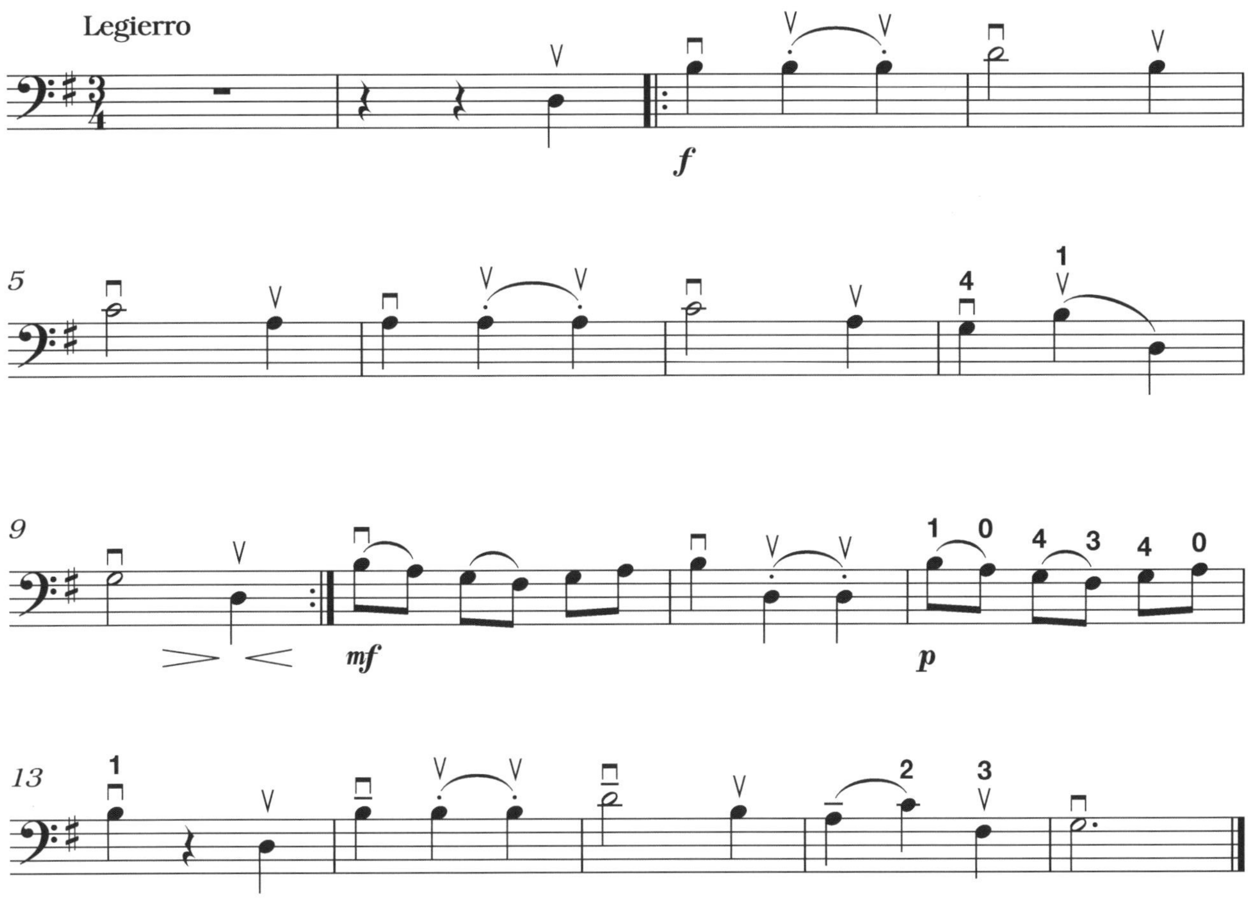

Bowing Practice

Use your whole bow on the half notes. Use half your bow on each quarter note. First, practice stopping your bow completely between the two quarter notes. Then practice making a gentle separation between the two notes. Play on all strings.

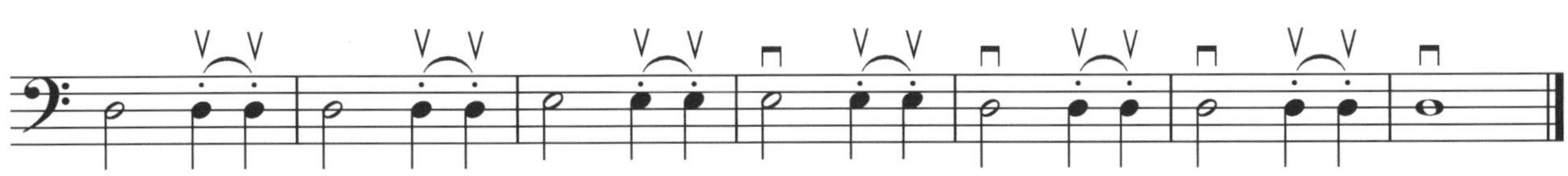

The Dancing Dog

A cello can only play two notes at a time, so a chord on the cello is played two notes at a time. First you play the bottom two notes, then you play the top two notes. The middle note is always heard.

Giocoso con spirito

Christine Watts

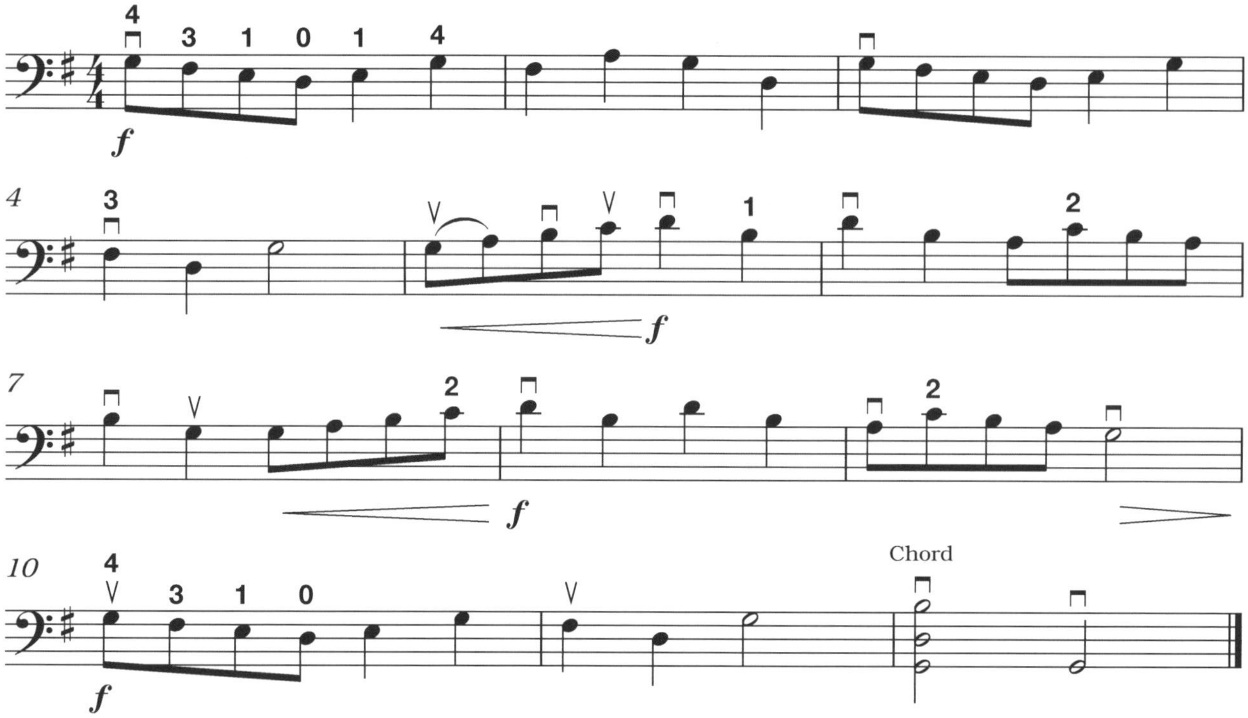

Between the Ox and the Donkey

American Folk Song

Andante misterioso

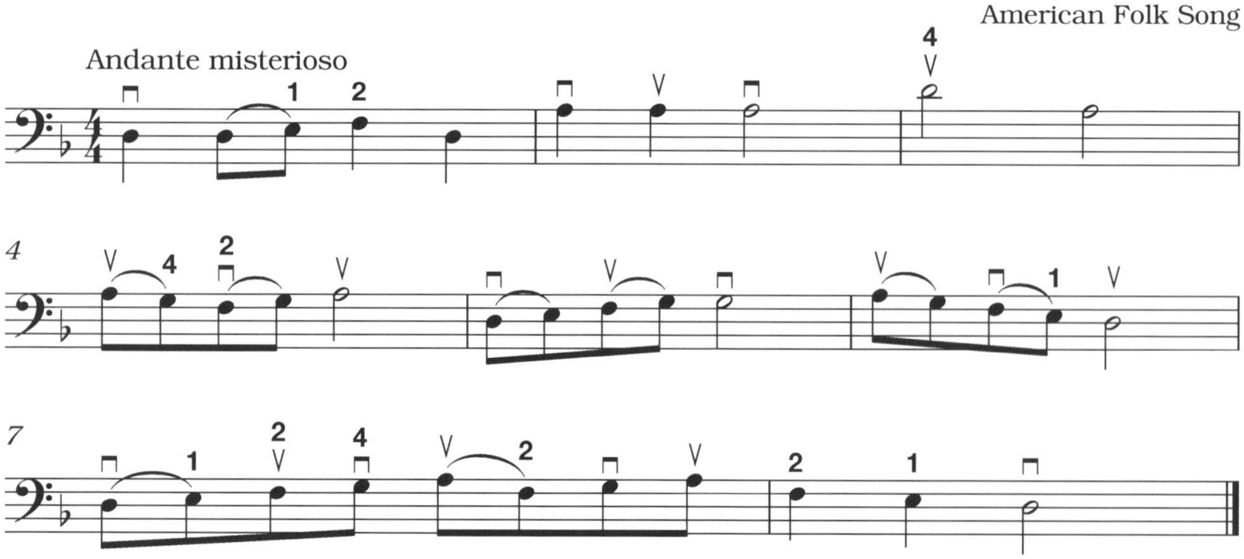

Country Fair Day

Christine Watts

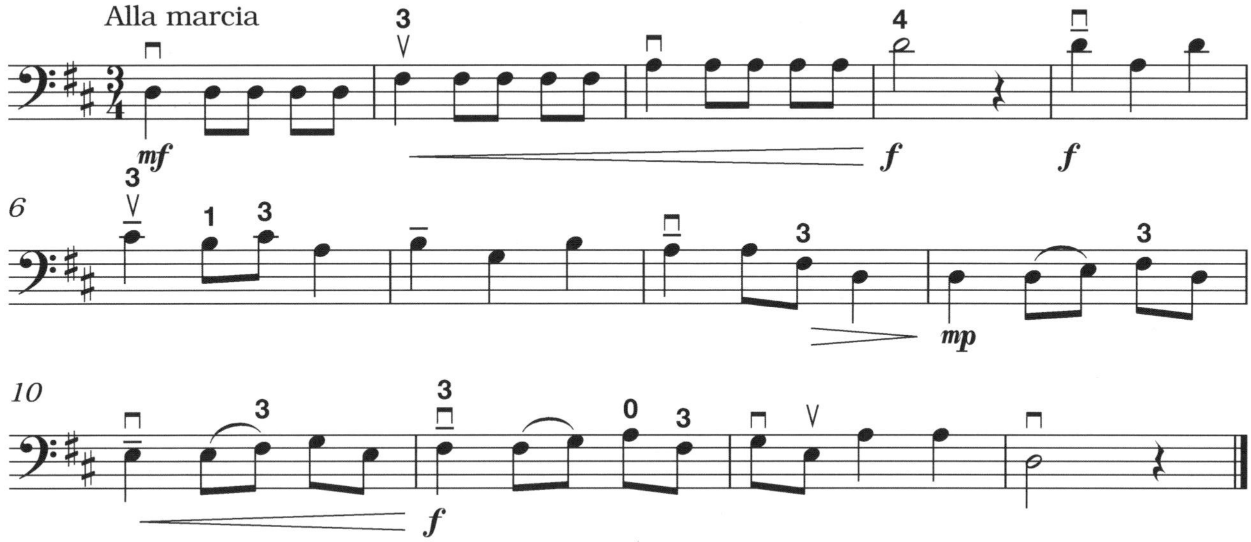

A fermata looks like this 𝄐. If you see one over a note, it means you can hold the note extra long for expression.

The Little Fiddle

American Folk Song

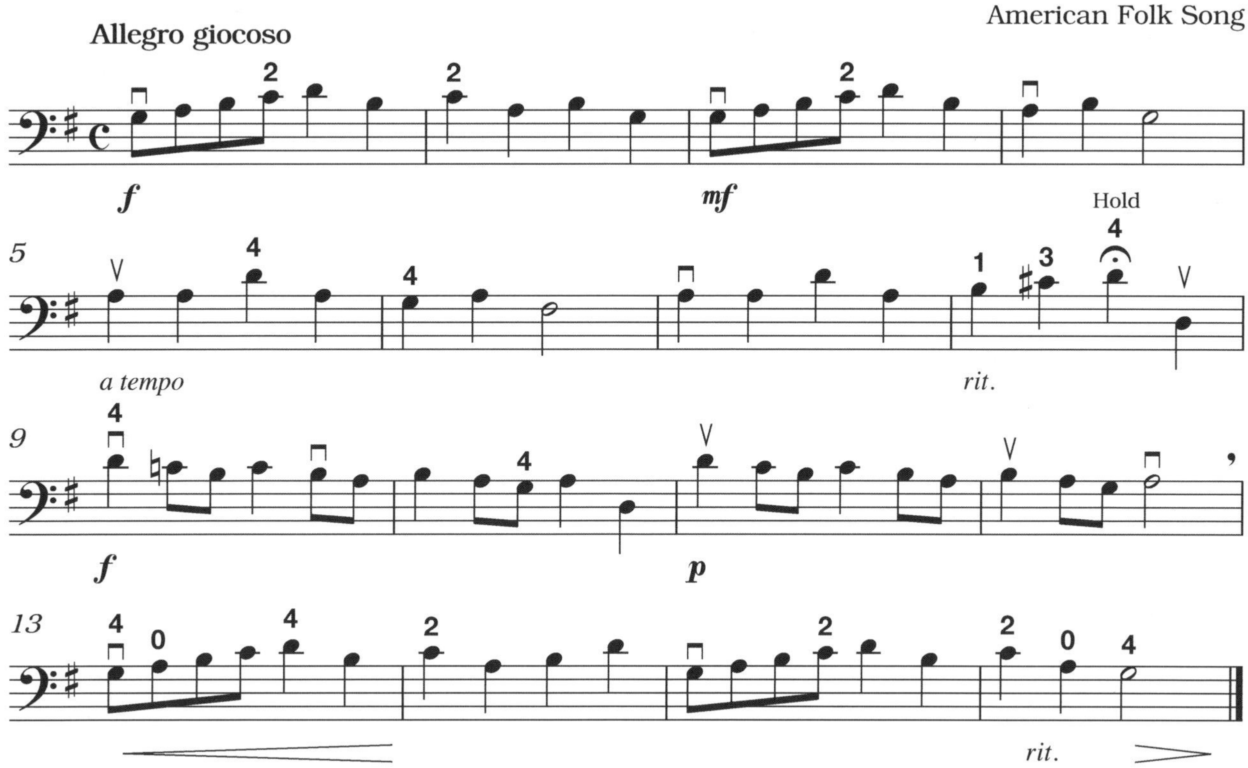

𝄒 means take a short pause. This can be for different reasons. Many times it is used for musical expression, or in this case it gives you time to take a double down bow.

Dotted quarter notes can be a little difficult to understand because they get 1½ beats. You beat twice on the dotted quarter note because it is the first beat plus the first half of the second beat. Count 1 and 2 on the quarter note, then say "and" on the next note, usually an ⅛ note.

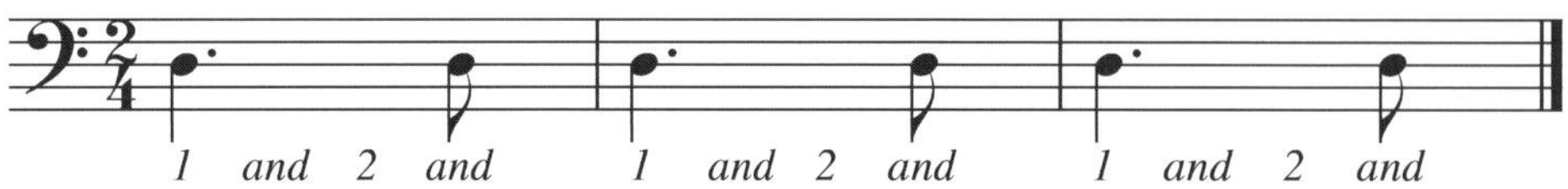

You can also say just *1, 2 and 1, 2 and*

Evening Song

Welsh Air

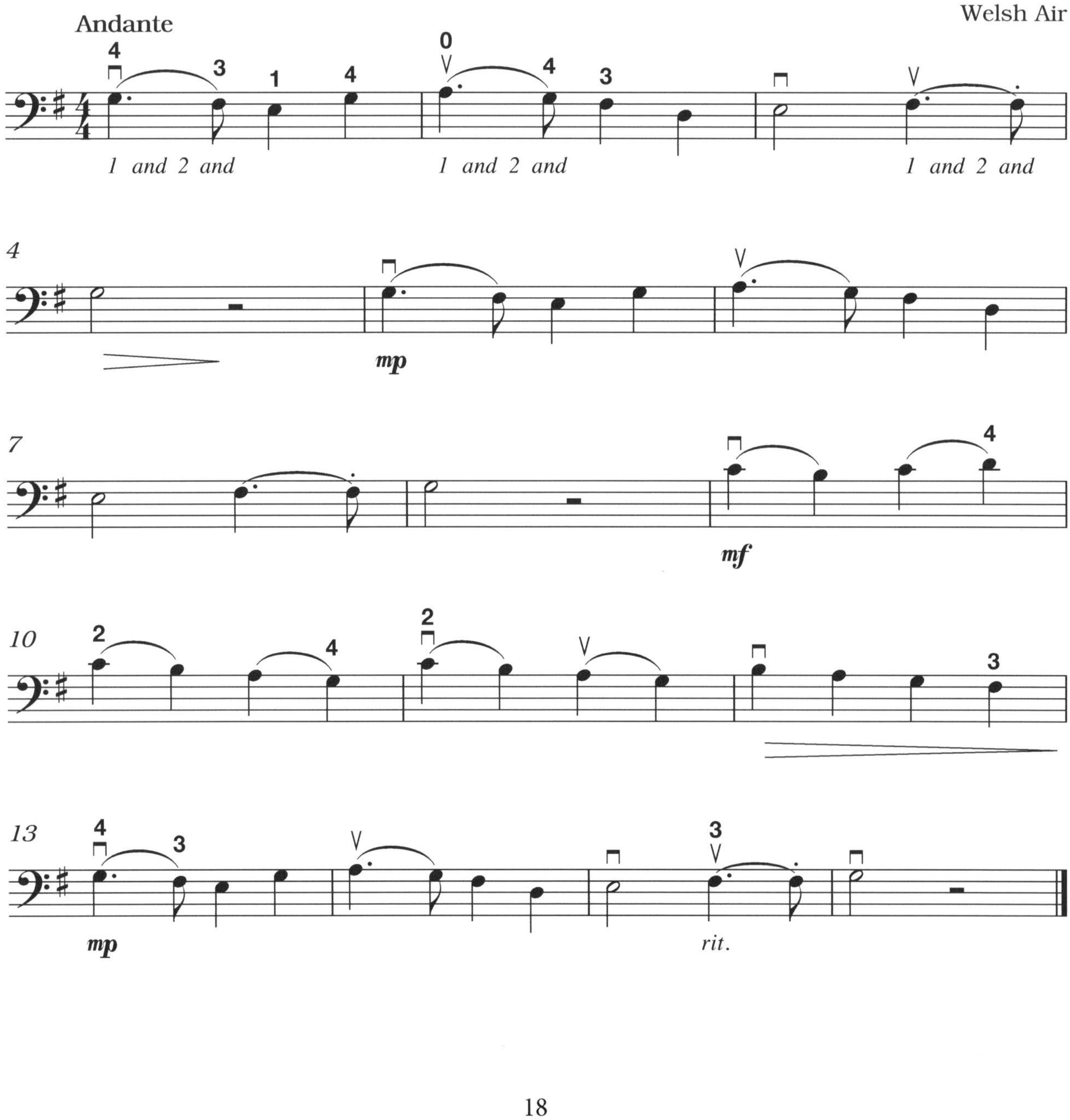

Eine Klein Nachtmusik

W. A. Mozart

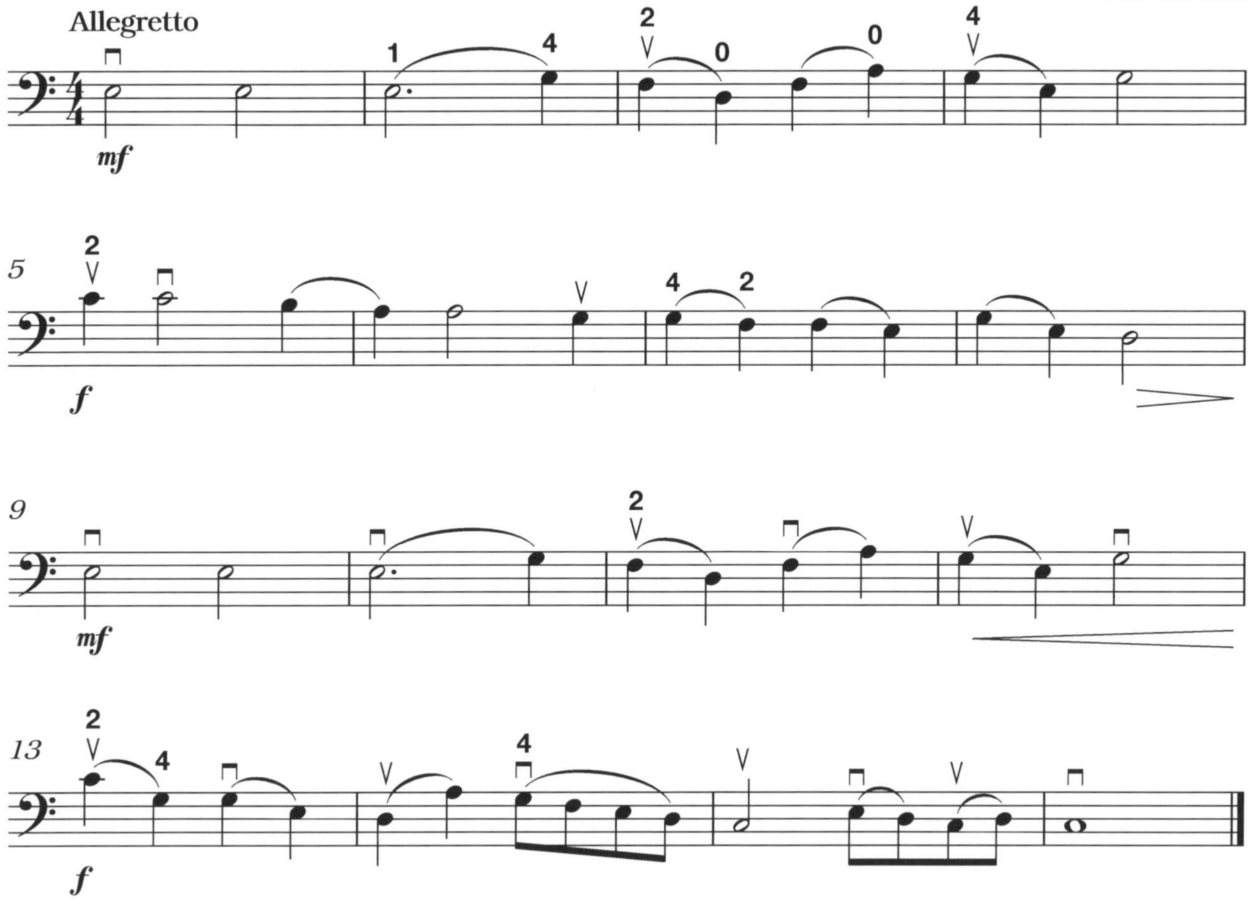

Barnyard Secrets

Christine Watts

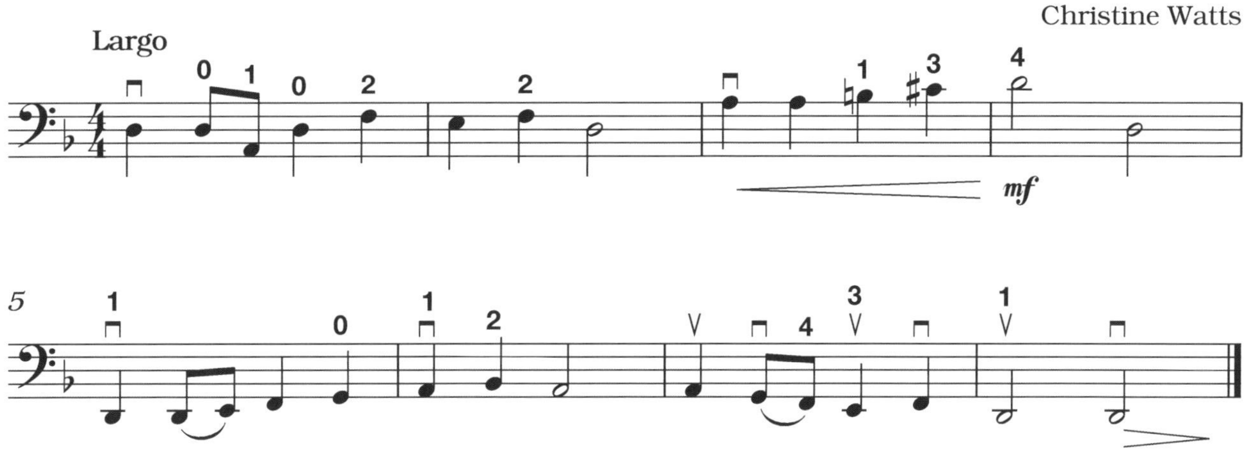

German Dance

Moderato, Energico

W. A. Mozart

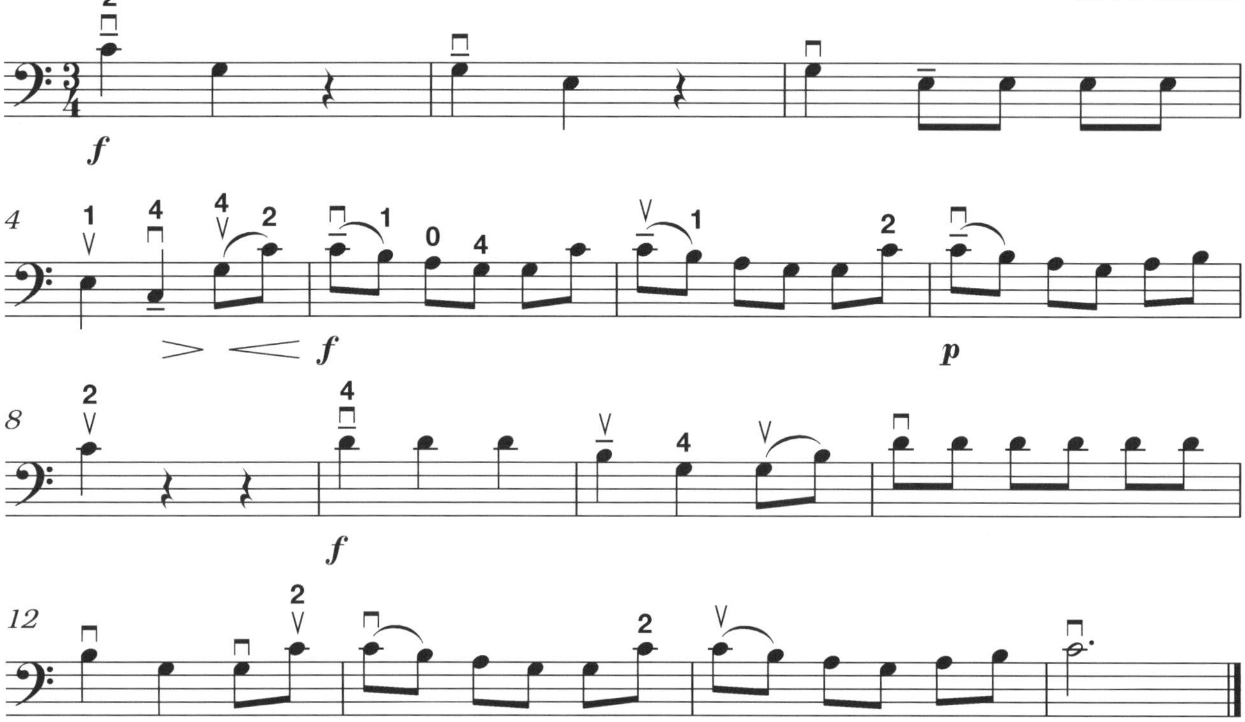

The Cool, Clear Pond

Andante, Tranquilo

American Folk Song

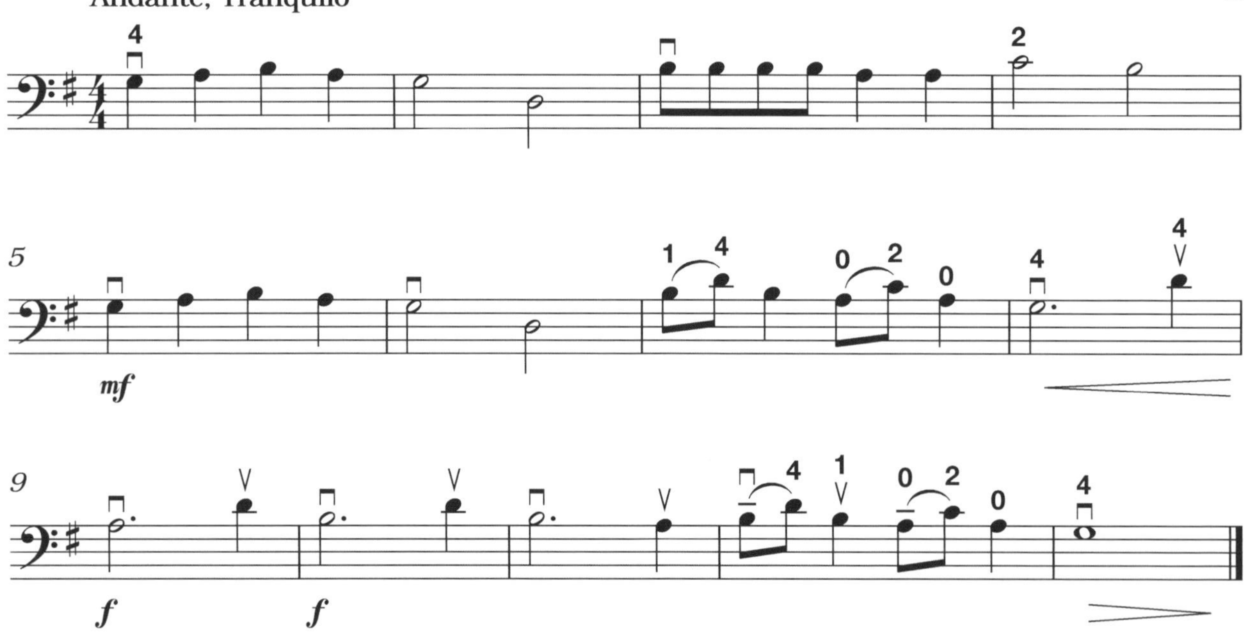

A Tie is two or more of the same note in a row connected with a slur. There are no lines or dots over the notes because they are very smooth. To play the low C♯, fingers 2, 3 and 4 need to reach out. Then finger four can play the C♯.

Beautiful Dreamer

Stephen Foster

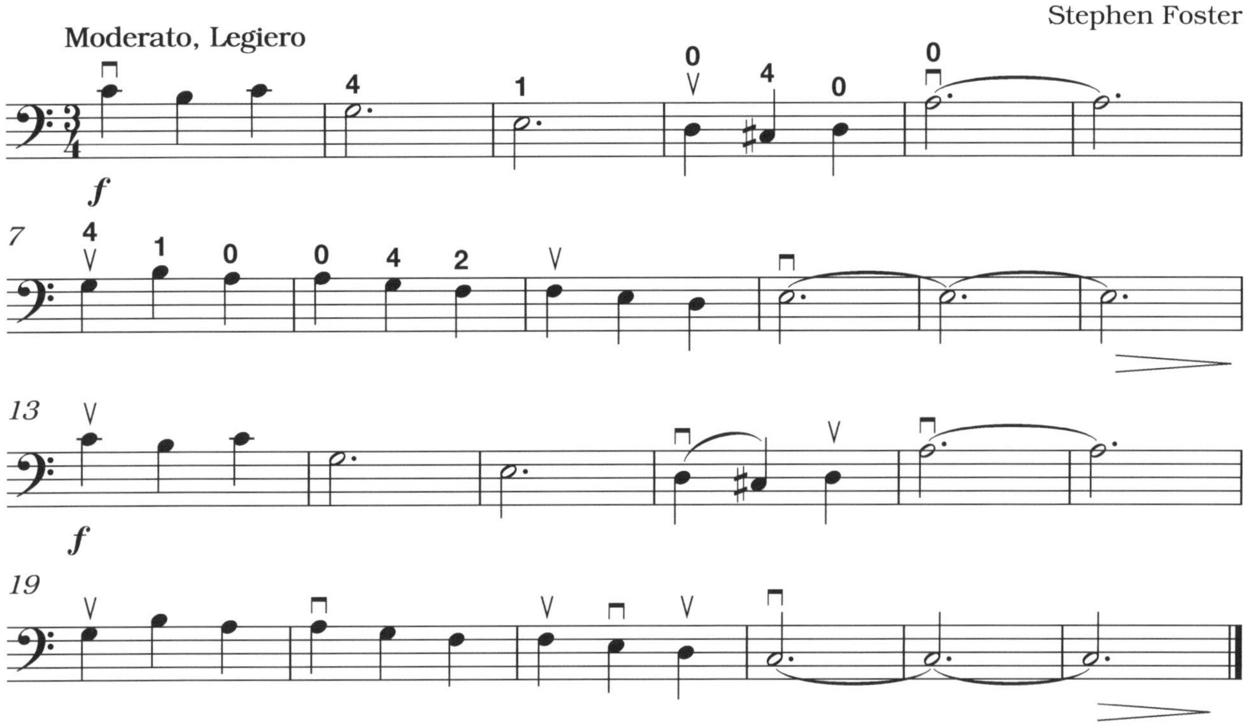

Eighth note triplets are 3 notes in a beat joined together by a beam. In these triplets each note gets 1/3 of the beat. They are faster than regular eighth notes because there are three notes in the beat instead of two. Often there is a 3 underneath the notes to show that they are a triplet.

Come and Dance With Me

Christine Watts

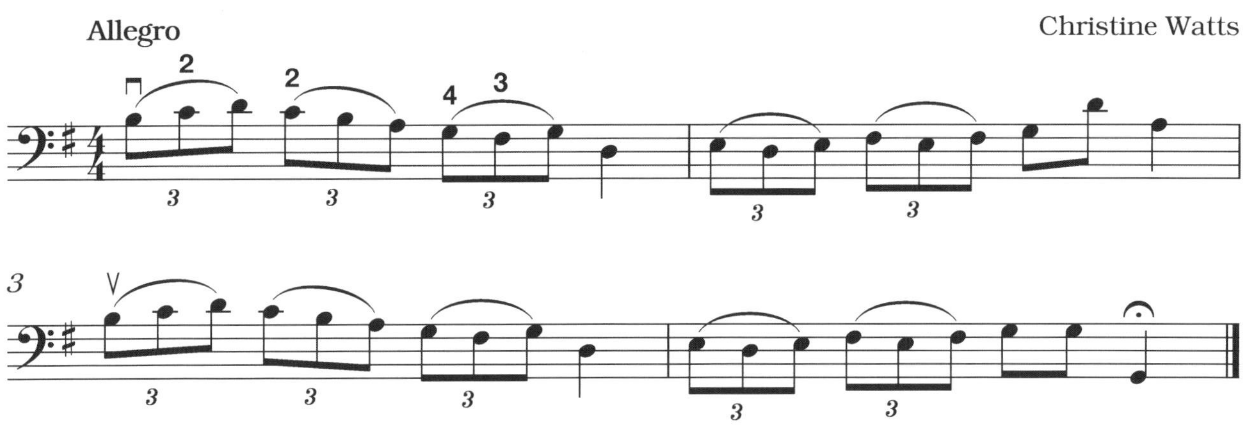

German Dance

Joseph Haydn

Allegro Moderato

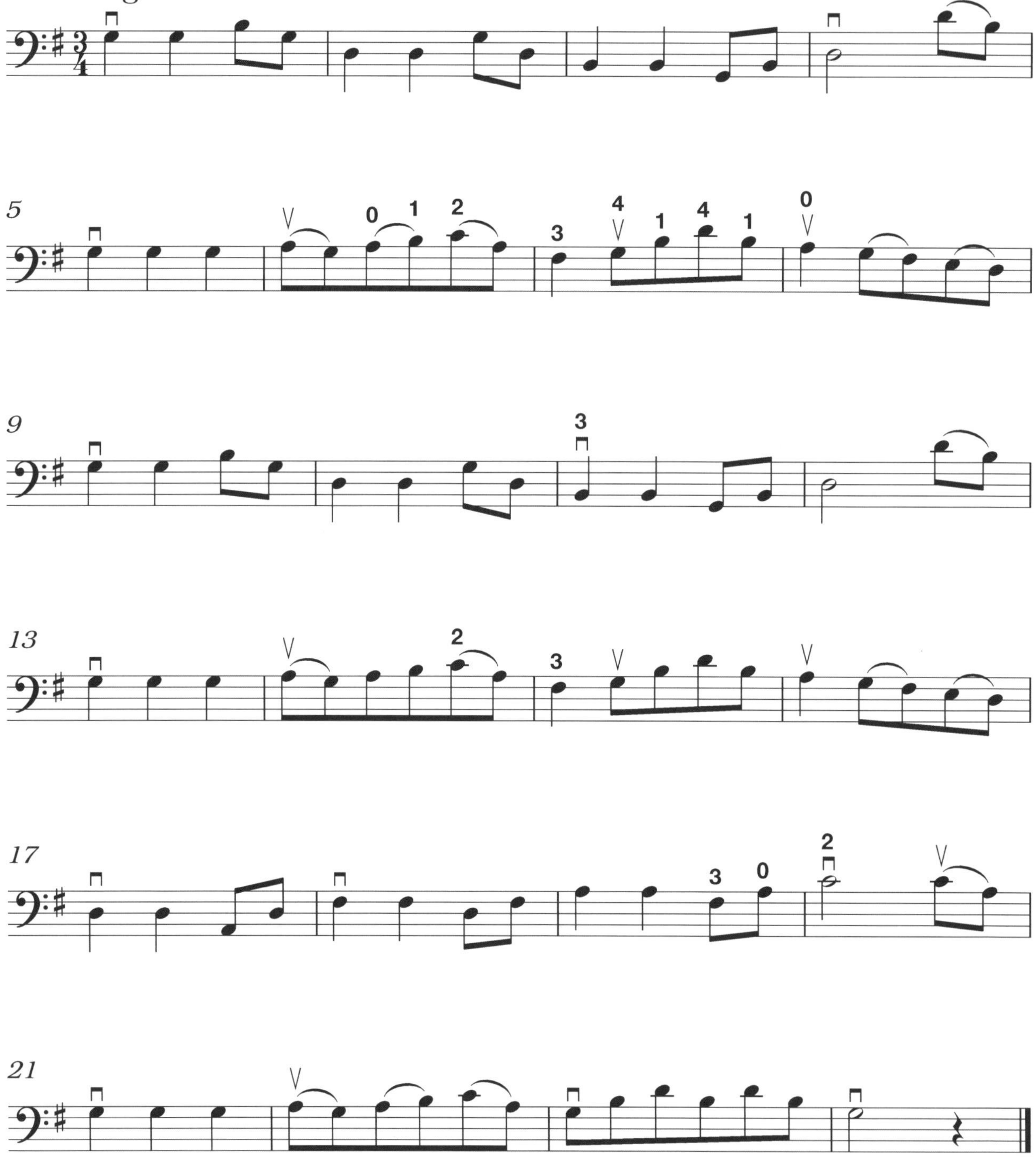

Song of Thanksgiving

Eduard Kremser

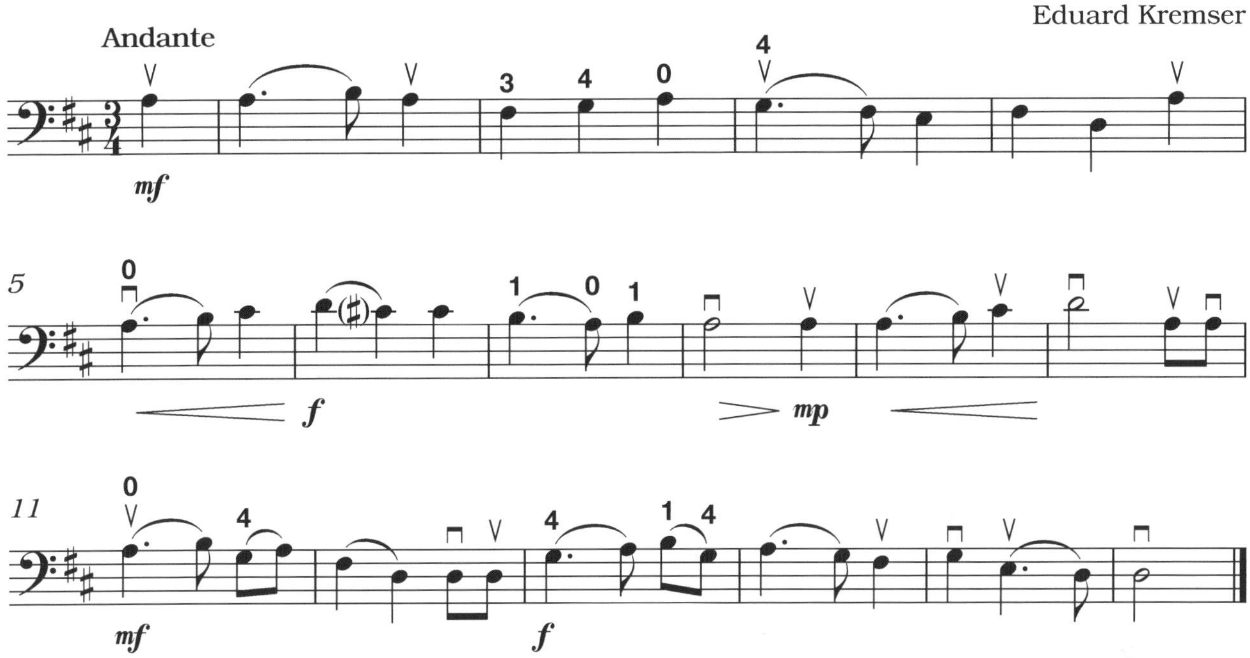

The Three Horsemen

German Folk Song

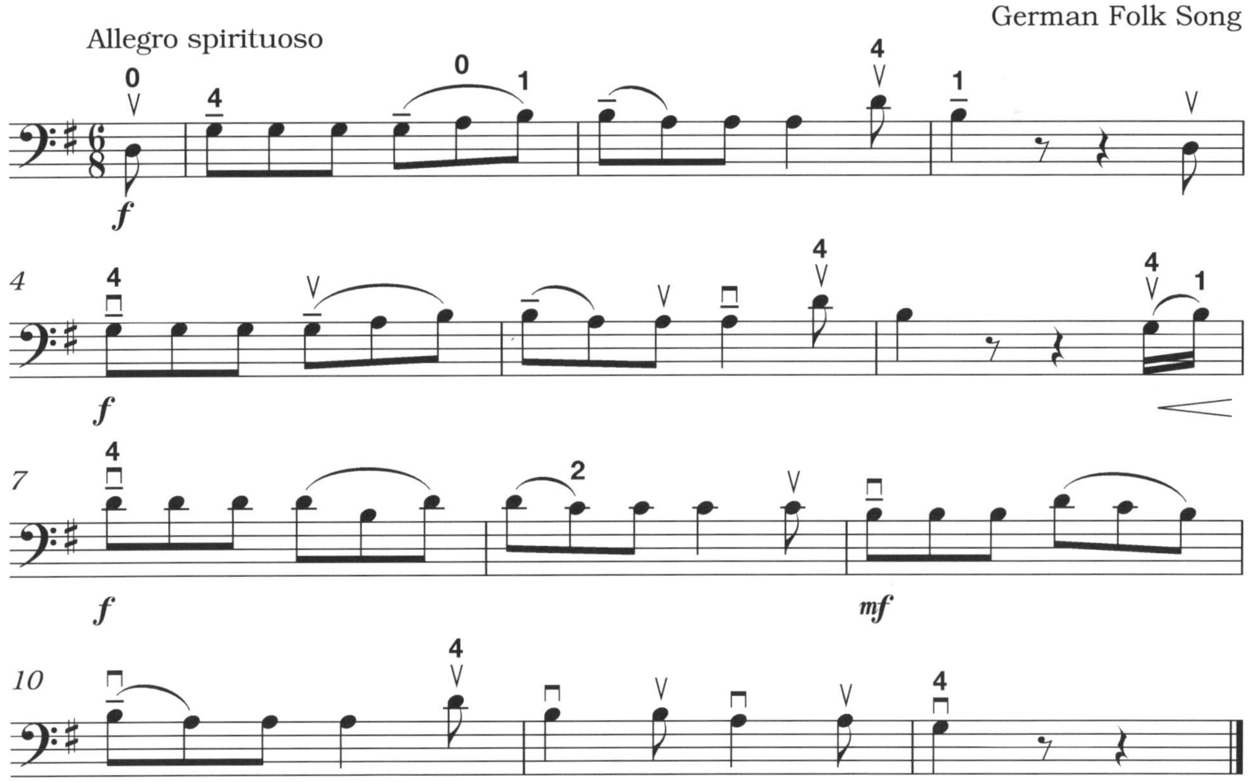

Stretching for Flats

To play B♭ or any first finger flat, reach your first finger almost straight back. Don't pull your hand back. Just move your first finger, keep fingers 2, 3, and 4 over their notes.

Stretch Position Exercise

Play on all strings.

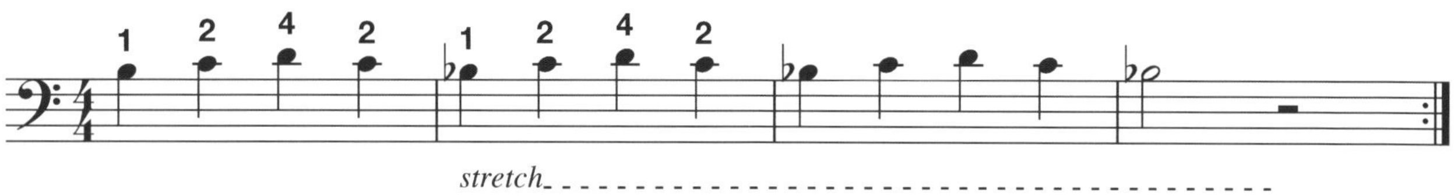

Little Flower

You can stay in stretch position for the entire song.

Christine Watts

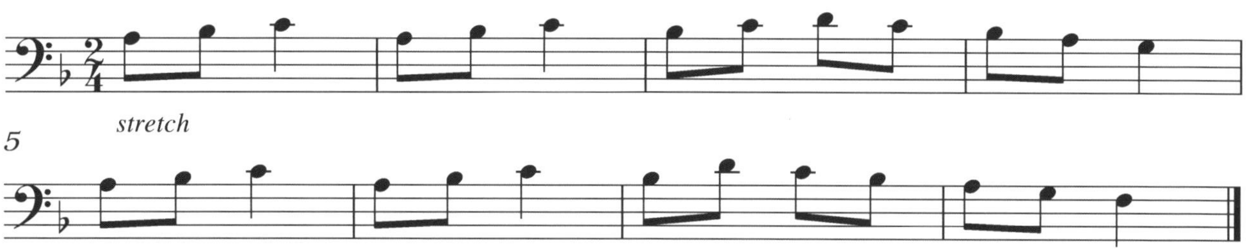

The Cuckoo and the Donkey

Allegro

C. F. Zelter

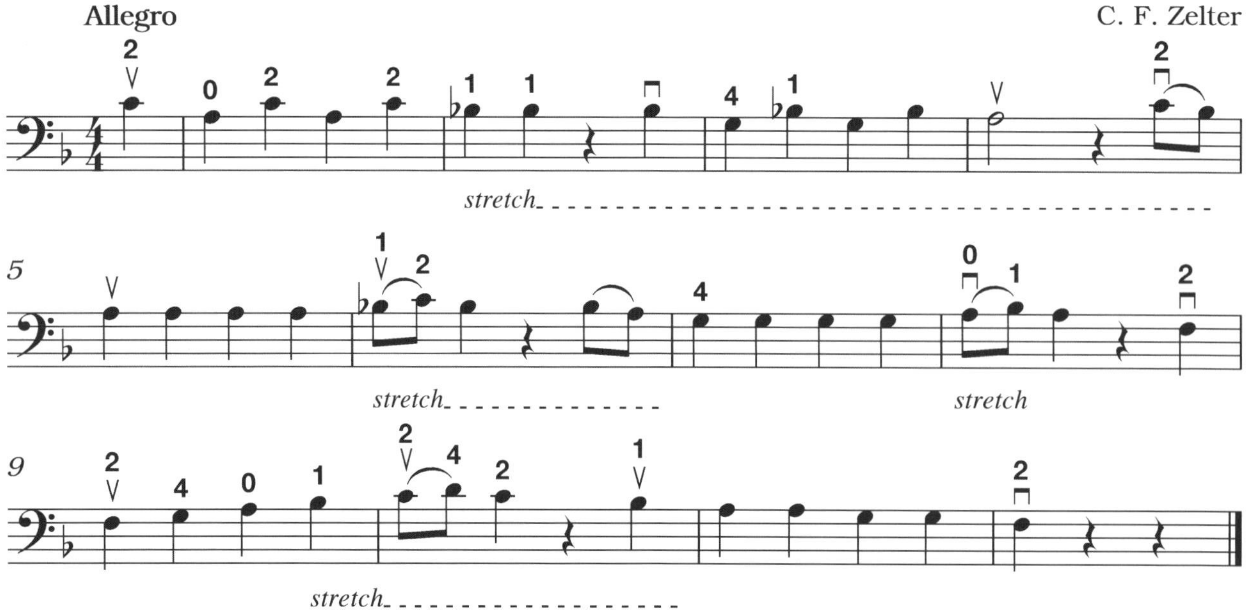

Song of the Sea

Christine Watts

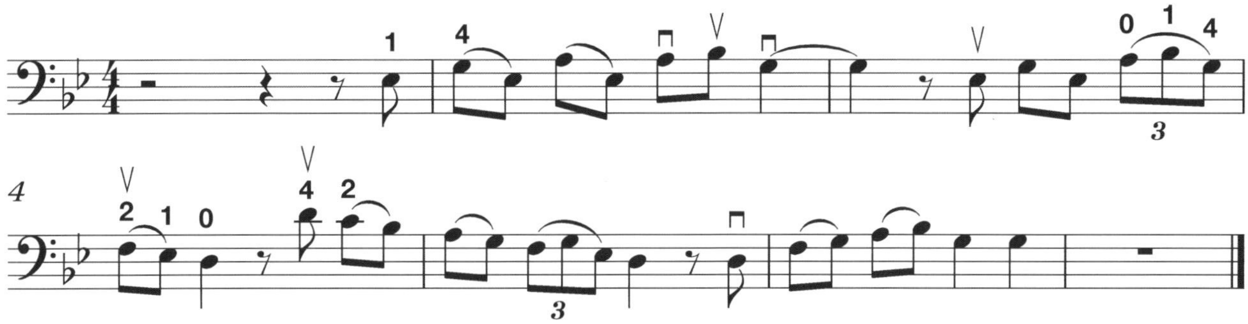

Home on the Range

Brewster Higley and Daniel E. Kelley

Andantino

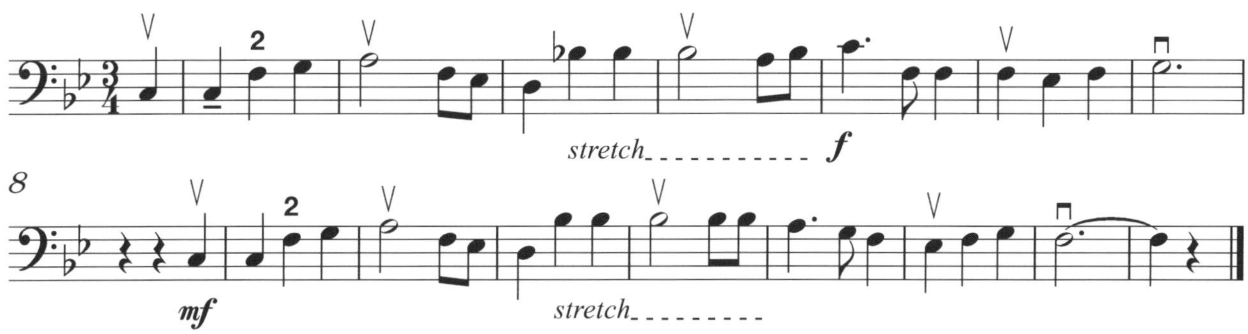

The Wind

Christine Watts

Allegro con moto agitato

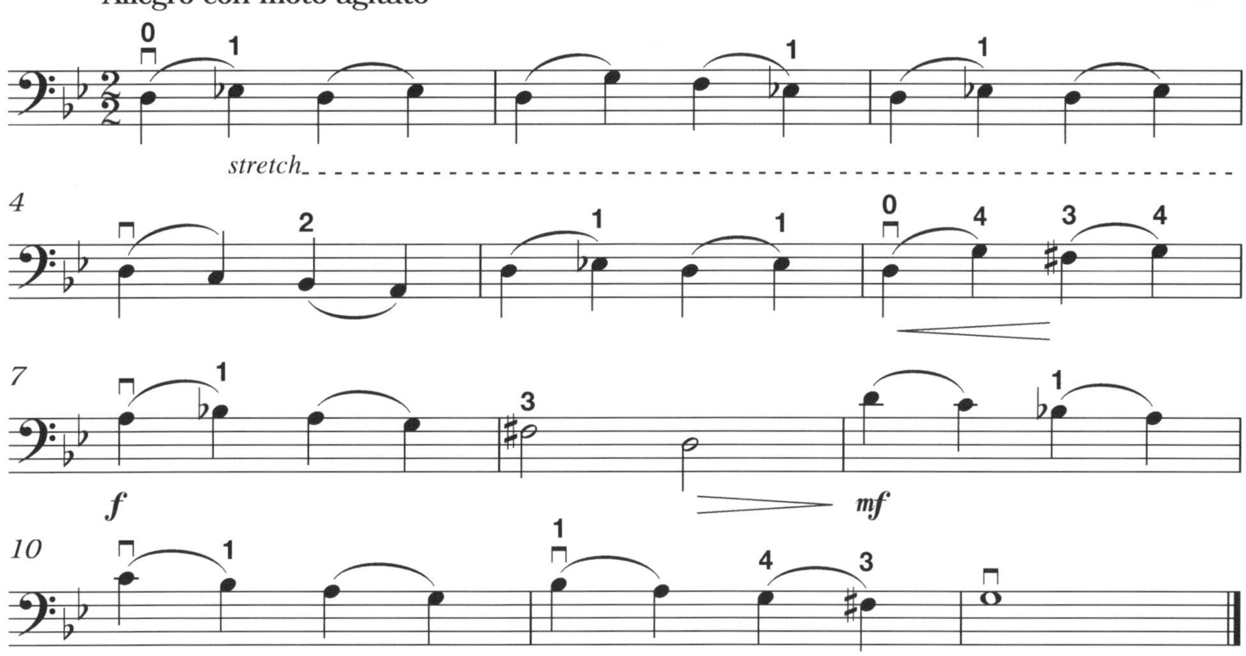

Stretch Position for Sharps

To stretch for sharps, reach every finger but your first out one note. 2nd finger goes where your 3rd finger was, 3rd finger goes where your 4th finger was, then 4th finger can reach a new note. A 4th finger sharp usually means stretch position.

Stretch Position Exercise

Play on all strings.

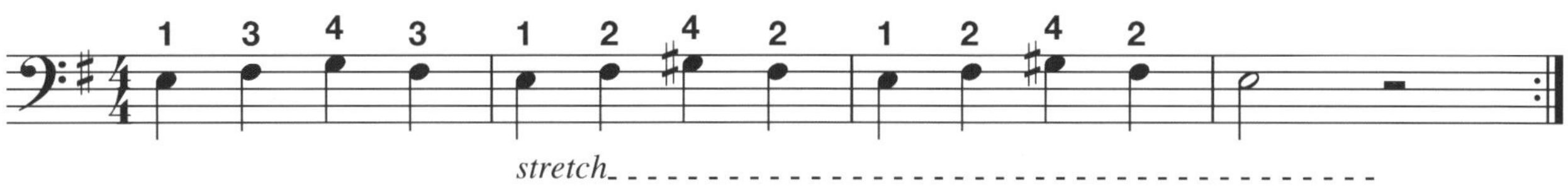

The Nut Tree

Old English Song

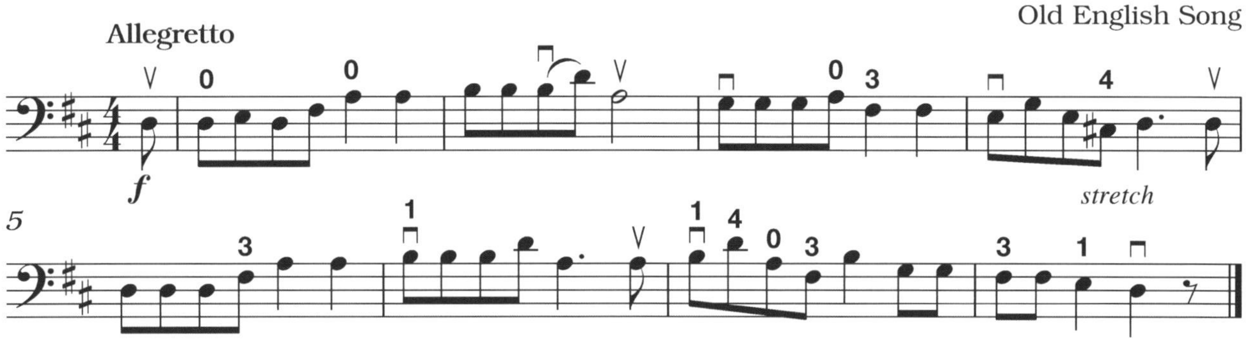

French Folk Song

You can stay in stretch position for the entire song.

Folk Song

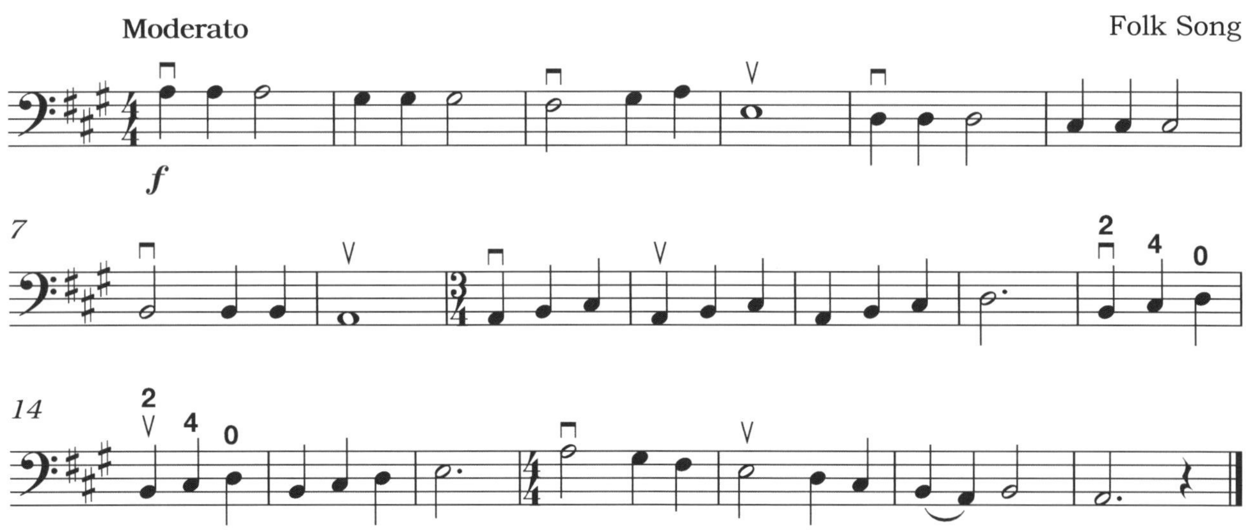

Hop, Hop, Hop

Traditional American

Andante

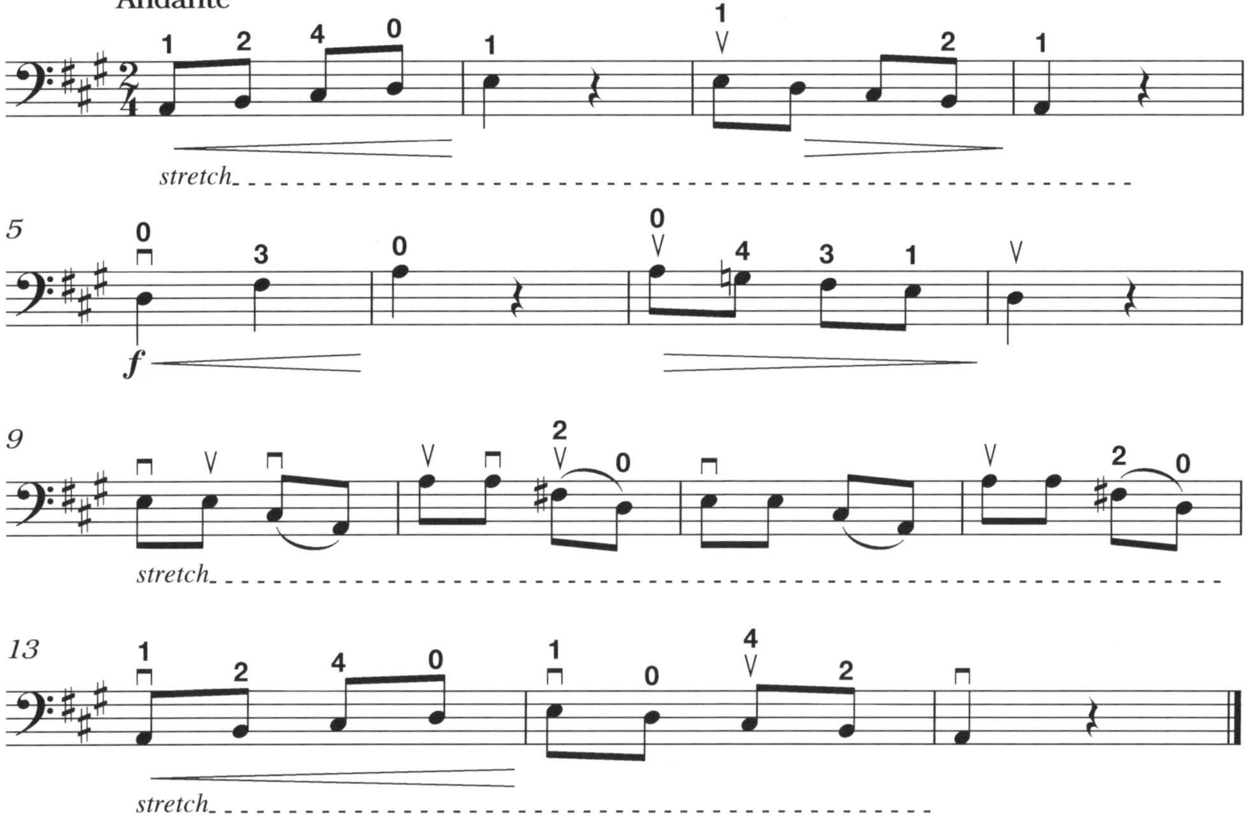

Sweet Betsy from Pike

American Folk Song

Allegretto

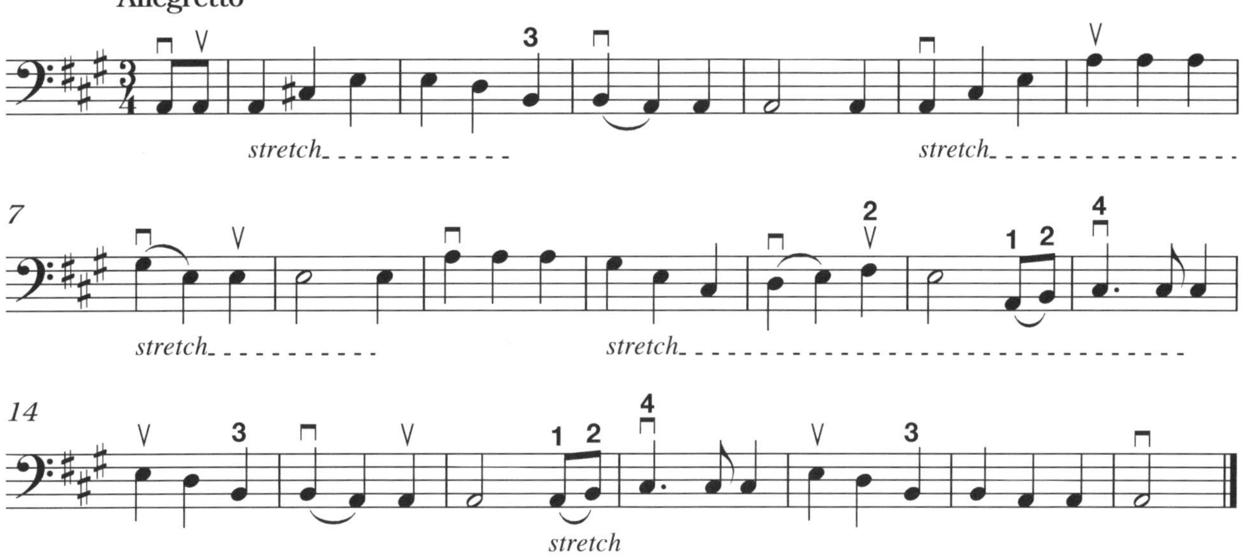

The Dancing Gazelle

Giocoso grazioso

Johann Kirnberger

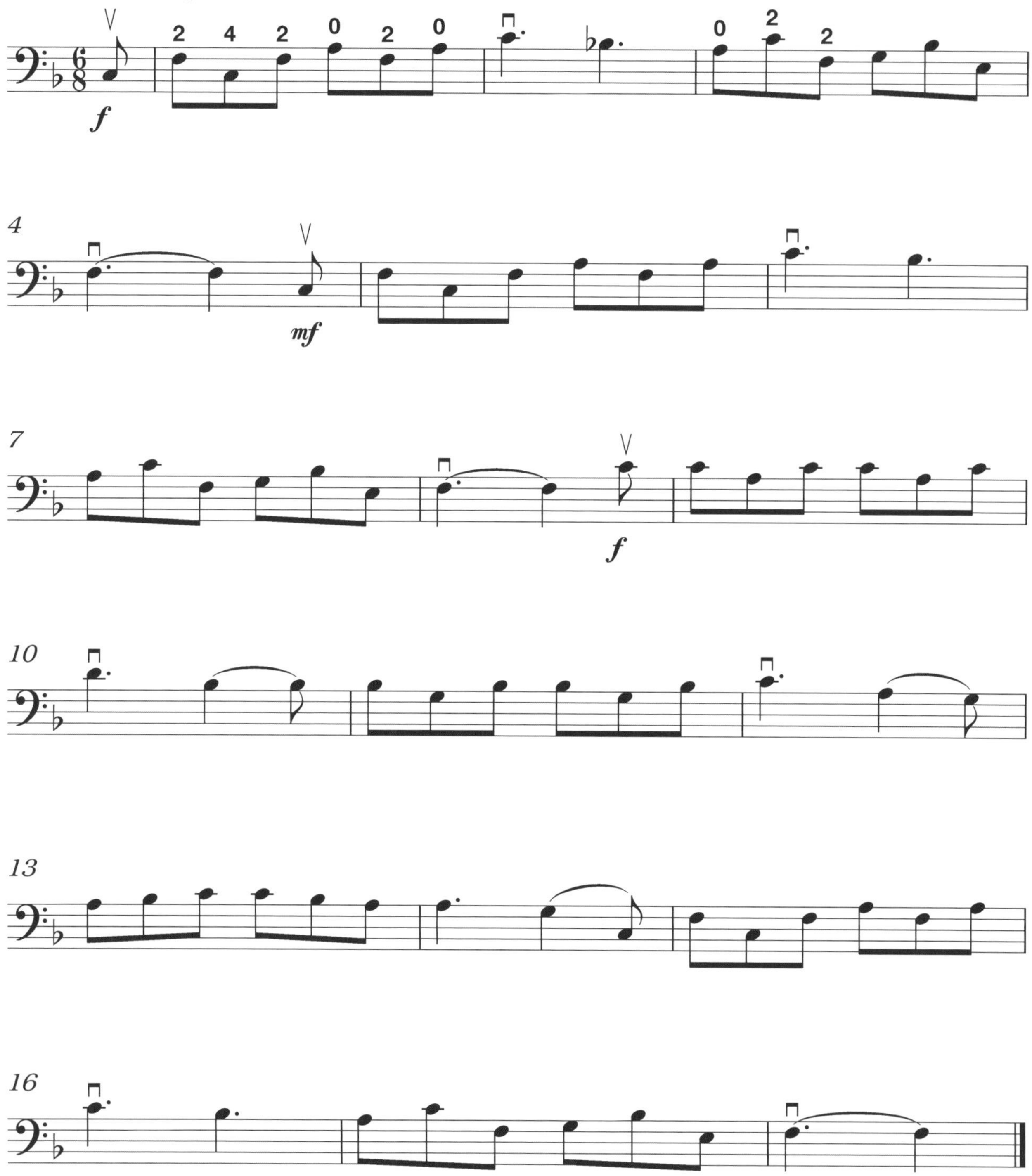

The Graceful Giraffe

17th Century Dance

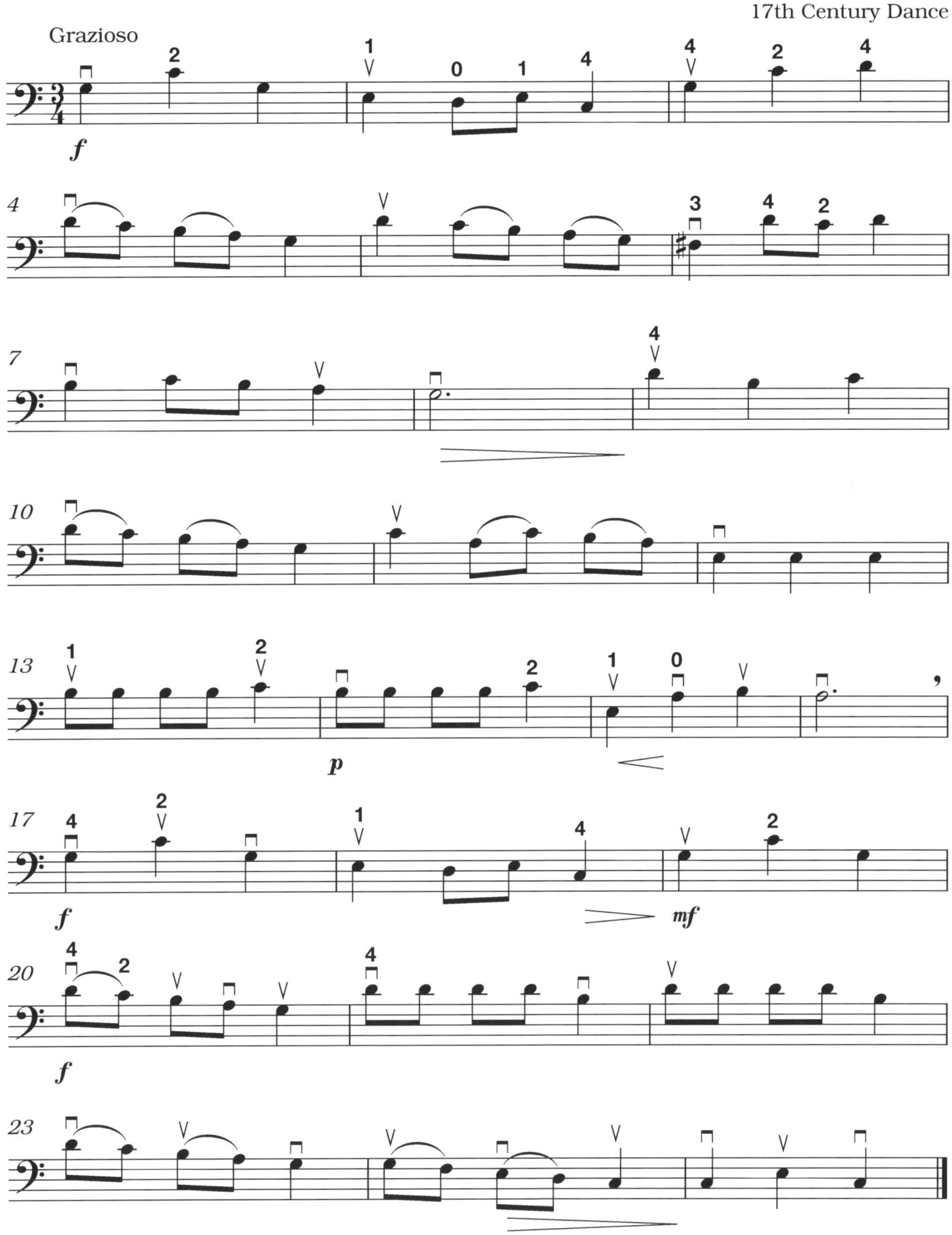

The Jumping Jackrabbit

Giocoso con spirito

Daniel Turk

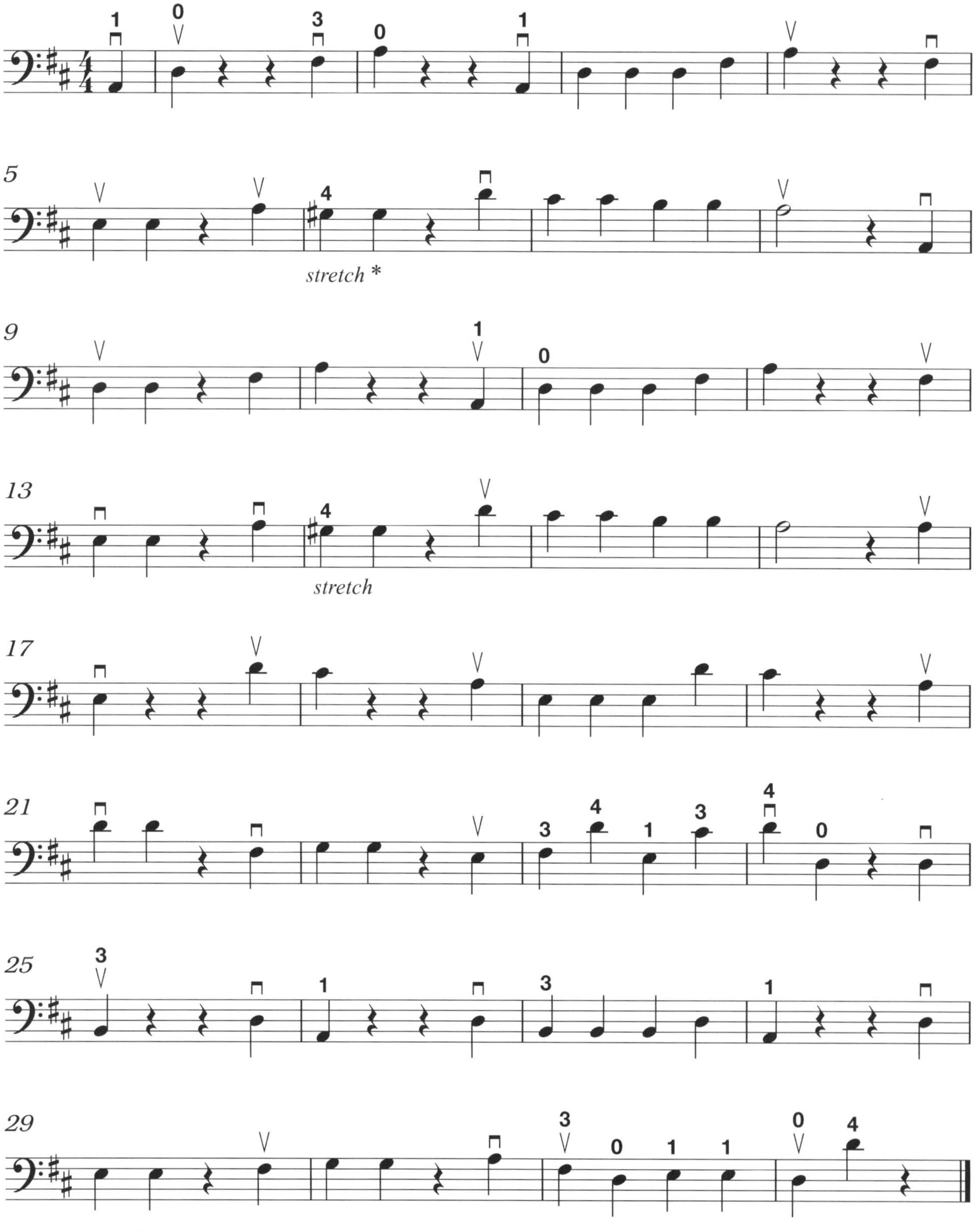

King of the Forest

Maestoso con brio

Christine Watts

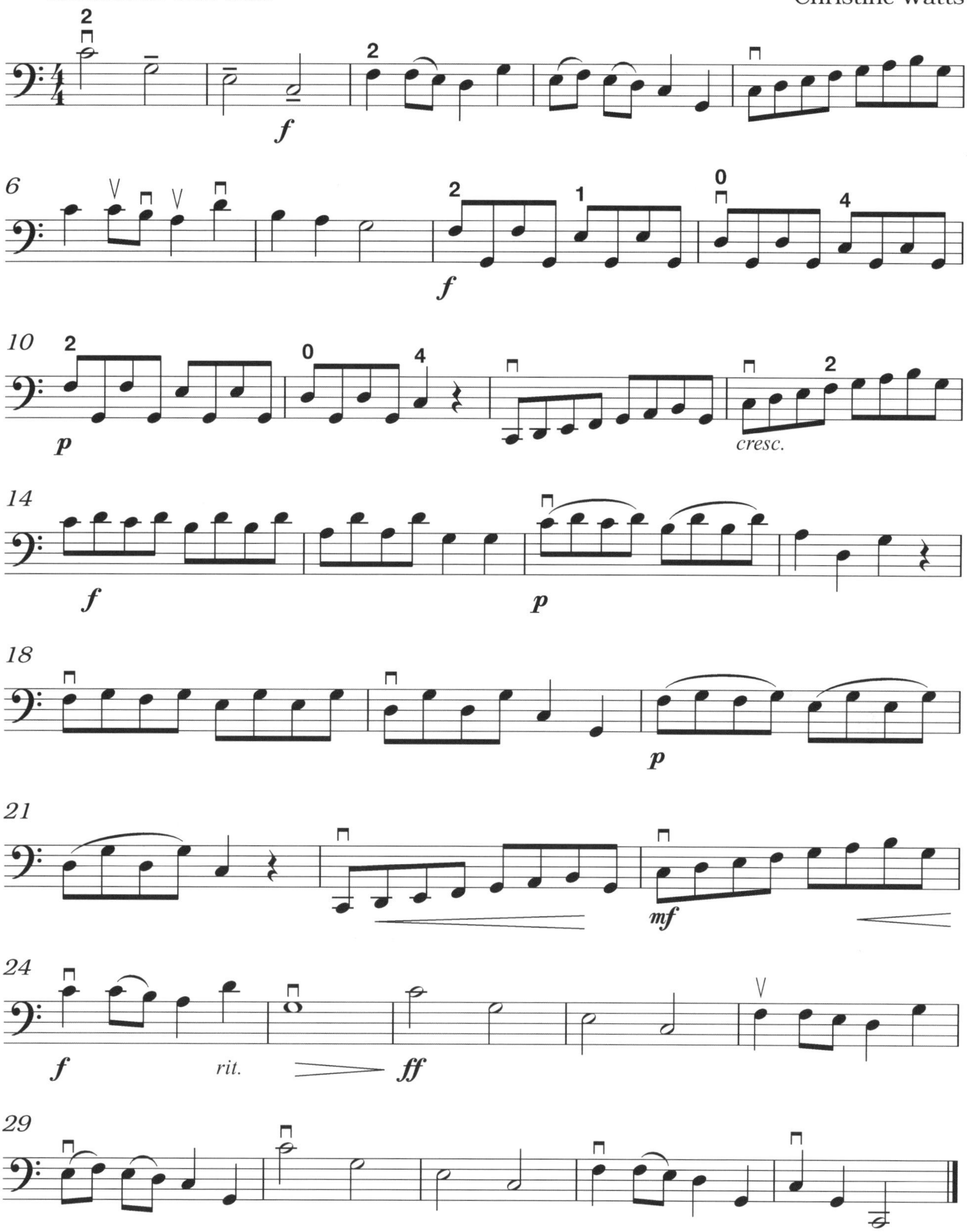

About the Author

Christine Watts is a graduate of the Curtis Institute of Music. As a young competition winner, she played solo twice with the Philadelphia Orchestra, and other well-respected orchestras. Her teaching career began at the New School of Music in Philadelphia PA with the renowned Curtis String Quartet. For years, Ms. Watts worked closely with the great cellist and teacher Orlando Cole. Currently, she works as a freelance musician and continues her teaching at the Wayne Art Center in Wayne PA. Beyond performance and teaching, Ms. Watts is the author of several books published by Mel Bay including *Cello Method Volumes 1* and *2*, and *Classical Duets for the Cello.*